About the author

June 21st 1974 I arrived on the scene in Ipswich, Suffolk. Brought up for 20 years in a little village called Stratford St Mary on the Suffolk side of the Essex/Suffolk border. Spent 10 happy years at Ipswich School where my writing skills were 'honed' by the likes of Messieurs Goodhand and Prior... well, when I say 'honed', I had no idea then that I would be in fact writing a book, and I suppose Mr Goodhand would've thought the Rise and Fall of Ipswich Town Football Club would have been more of an apt title... and even then he'd have probably still given it a D!

At the time of writing I am 22 years old, and am still buzzing from four years of amazing experiences. After completing 'A' Levels I took a year out and went travelling around the world with my long time school friend Tony. This was our first big trip – probably similar to any that a reader of this book may be about to do. We plodded off out via America, Hawaii, Fiji, then a fantastic few months in Australia. The return leg was a mixture of the delights of the Far East, as we hopped back over Indonesia, Singapore, Malasia and Thailand, before returning back to Blighty! My next real experience was a Christmas spent out in Russia in a place called Perm, fairly close to Siberia. This was a cold and chilling experience of the fall of Communism and the break up of the USSR. I was there because of a Russian girlfriend, whose treatment of me almost matched the -40 degree temperatures, and which subsequent break-up prompted a trip next summer to North America as an escape from the dark traces of Siberia that still remained in my blood! This trip saw me hitch-hike solo over 5,000 miles across Canada, and then travel down into America, visiting friends at Universities and others working on the infamous 'kids camps'. South America is next on the list.

I have just graduated from Manchester University, getting a 2:1 in Economics. I busk on the street (Colchester, Ipswich and Plymouth) with my didgeridoos, and raise money for the Essex Voluntary Association for the Blind, for whom I have just run the 1997 London Marathon. If you like 'dige' music you can buy *On the Street* by me (In'dige'nous) for a fiver – now working on a CD.

So in a brief nutshell  of man about town, with loads of d[...] e else... and if you see me, why not [...] reat laugh, but more importantly to [...] e. School and University equipped [...] qualifications, however travelling ma[...] erson, and has fitted me with a personality and the social skills for being active in life.

Mum and Dad
Did you want me to go?
I didn't know,
But I went.
You didn't stop me,
Were you proud?
I came back,
To your relief.
I had changed,
For the better,
…my life had begun.

Before You Go

Gap year advice - tips & hints for first-time travellers

Tom Griffiths

Foreword by
Michael Palin

Quiller Press
London

Dedicated to:
Mum and dad who have eventually resigned to my itchy feet, Claire for her amazing support and encouragement... and of course Tony, who accompanied my first steps, and from where it all began.

Tom's Disclaimer
I have written this book with the view that you are not penguins, but intelligent young people. Therefore I expect everything I talk about to be taken with a pinch of salt, and any decisions you take to be of your own free will. If you choose to run off a cliff, under a bus, or marry a nun – it's not my fault, and so I take no responsibility for your actions. Act on my advice as you wish, but you can't blame me for your actions.

Although I make every effort to ensure the accuracy of all of the information in this book, changes occur incessantly. I cannot therefore take responsibility for facts, addresses and circumstances in general that are constantly subject to alteration.

Now... get on with reading the book!

'A journey of a thousands miles must begin with a single step.'
Lao Tzu, Chinese Philosopher.

You've just taken it.

Copyright © 1997 Tom Griffiths
First published 1997 by
Quiller Press Limited
46 Lillie Road
London SW6 1TN

ISBN 1 899163 33 6

Designed by Jo Lee
Cartoons by Dave Upson
Cover photo by Darren Bell
Printed by Biddles Ltd

Contents

Foreword by Michael Palin   *vii*
Author's preface   *viii*
A quick point about reading the book   *ix*
Chapter 1 – **So why travel?**   1
Chapter 2 – **Decisions**   5
Chapter 3 – **Packing**   18
Chapter 4 – **Parents**   32
Chapter 5 – **Health and Emergencies**   46
Chapter 6 – **Male solo**   54
Chapter 7 – **Female solo**   61
Chapter 8 – **Going with a friend**   75
Chapter 9 – **Safety**   84
Chapter 10 – **Money and finances**   92
Chapter 11 – **Hitch-hiking**   111
Chapter 12 – **Tips, hints, and problems**   120
Chapter 13 – **Coming home**   153

Appendix 1 – **Things to do check list**   157
Appendix 2 – **Good books on the market**   162
Appendix 3 – **Useful addresses, telephone numbers
                 and information**   163

Acknowledgements   174
Subject index   175
Voucher pages   177

Picture courtesy of Fane Brown

by
Michael Palin

I was once taken to task for being obsessed with toilets and bowel movements in my television documentaries. I make no apologies for being a toilets before temple traveller. Too often travel is presented as a series of glamourous getaway moments, glorious sunsets, colourful markets, elegant buildings and sublime contemplations of the beauties of creation.

These may well be the sort of things that make us want to set out in the first place, but such pleasures are subjective. One traveller can find sublime happiness on a Polish cargo boat, another on the rim of a volcano, another in a Mayan temple.

What the departing traveller needs to know is not so much other people's opinions of what's wonderful, but basic, unromantic, mundane and absolutely essential advice on how to get to these wonderful things and what to do when you get there and find you have diahorrea, sunburn and no money to get back.

This is why I think Tom Griffiths's book is useful and valuable and quite possibly indispensable. It is a treasure-trove of helpful information for young travellers (and old ones too). It's clear, comprehensive and written with wisdom and humour. It has answers to just about every question you could and should ask before setting out. He even has a section called Coming Home – the first time I've seen this interesting phenomenon dealt with in any travel guide. It is a real problem as I discovered on my return from going Around the World in Eighty Days. I found myself shunned at parties – after all, what do you say to someone who's just been round the world? If you have the urge to travel you should read this book – before, during and after you go – AND it makes wonderful toilet paper.

Author's Preface

"Travel teaches toleration" Benjamin Disraeli (1832)

Every once in a while journalism portrays backpacking to be dangerous, and then in the same breath reports that Elvis is alive and running a chippy in Peckham. Make of it what you will!

So what is this book about?

Hi there!

Well, most importantly I have recently been in the position that you are in now... you're apprehensive, daunted by the whole thought of actually going away to distant places, and possibly confused as to how to approach it all, i.e. what tickets to buy, backpack to take, insurance to get, etc., etc., etc.

Yet on the other hand you are, deep down, excited about the prospect of taking time out to 'discover the world', and in doing so discover more about yourself. The more you hear stories from people who have 'been there, done that', the more you want to go... suddenly they're not travel bores any more, but 'Gurus' who give you visions of tropical islands and fun in the sun! Well it's all out there waiting for you, you've just got to *go for it!*

A great authority on the subject of travel?... not me, I'm just 'Tom'!

Because I am talking about real events, I mention people by name. Friends of mine such as Tony – my first travelling partner, Tim – a school friend, Colin – a Uni mate, cousin Helena, and various people here and there. They are mentioned on the odd occasion to add relevance to a point. Unfortunately for them, 'names have not been changed to protect the innocent', and so humiliation may be the outcome. All I have to say to that is... tough! These and other friends have contributed their advice to this guide.

☛ **We want to help you, as we ourselves have been helped. You can take our advice or leave it, but it will get you started before you go, give you ideas, make you think, and help you come up with some decisions.**

What will you get from this book?

We have all been in your position, all not really known what to do, and have asked advice from others... advice we have followed, practically to the letter. Most of it has been really useful, and the rest, well, as you can imagine... your Grandad telling you how to avoid sharks in the southern hemisphere (like he did during the war!)... really won't get you very far, fascinating though it is!

There is so much pathetic advice out there which is about as useful as Bernard Manning's 'Top Tips For Firm Buttocks'. People are even trying to give it to me to put in to this book... 'Don't forget to warn people that if they walk the streets of Sydney at night that they have a 1 in 3 chance of being attacked.' I mean... come on, give me a break!

☛ **You will not find this book jam packed with my thousand and one great travelling stories (to the great relief of my friends!)**

☛ **It is not a book telling you what to do and where to go in all the countries you may like to visit.**

For these simply look at the shelves bursting at the seams around you! Novels such as *On the Road* by Jack Kerouac, and the various Michael Palin books are perfect for whetting your appetite for travel stories and travel (look in the back under '**Some good books on the market**'). The Lonely Planet guide books are fantastic as guides for all the countries in which you wish to roam.

A QUICK POINT ABOUT READING THE BOOK...

Because there is so much that applies to everyone from 'across all the borders', I do advise you to read the book from cover to cover, and not skip out the bits about male travelling just because you are female, or vice versa. So much applies to both sexes that **I have written the book in a way that it is important to read all the way through**. If I had made it specific in parts it would have ended up as a long list of boring facts, figures and thoughts. I have therefore decided to bring up points in the various sections so as to make it more readable. Are you confused about what I am trying to say as I am? Ok, a few examples needed.

♦ In the section on **Parents** I bring up the issue of 'keeping in touch' whilst travelling, a few ideas, tips, etc., one of which is 'Post Restante'. Intrigued by this... then go and read about it!

♦ In the section on **Male Solo** I talk about a few personal experiences, 'culture shock', meeting people, travelling around, etc.

♦ And in **Female Solo**, I address thoughts about awareness of other cultures, work, etc.In the three points highlighted above there is something there for everyone, and they're written as part of a text that won't/shouldn't, send you to sleep. So to let the book do you justice, please read all the way through... it's not very long, and if I can do it, then you certainly have no excuse!

If you are aged 17-24 then you are at the perfect age to travel.

At the moment you have no real commitments. You may think you do, but unless you have a house, mortgage, two children, a spouse, car, job, debts and a dog called Gerald, you are not a fully fledged member of the 'rat race', and you won't be for another few years yet. However, once you get your membership card and enter it, then commitments make travel like this virtually impossible. You've got to do it now!

The same old routine... break from it!

There is a lot of pressure to follow routine, i.e. GCSE's, 'A' levels, university, job or any variation around that ... maybe starting work just after GCSE's or 'A' Levels. There is a worry about taking a year out for example, people worry about wasting time, but...

☛ **What is the difference between working 43 years instead of 44?**

Taking a year out before university?

◆   Lots of people do it, plus it gives you a well earned break between 4 years of working for exams, and another 3 (minimum).
◆   Remember that it is encouraged by Universities, as you are seen be be more mature and so ready for the challenges of higher education.
◆   It is also seen by others as the break between being a teenager and an adult.

The same applies for after university/College.

You are graduated, qualified... what for?
◆   Not too sure about what direction you want to go in (like me, right at this minute)?
◆   Need something to fill in all those blank bits on the CV and on the application forms?
◆   Want to become more employable?
◆   Or do you just need a break?

THEN GO!

I've harked on long enough... there's a world out there... go and see it, and live life to the full! So... if you need some friendly advice to help to kick the ball and start it rolling *Before you Go*

...THEN READ ON

CHAPTER I

So why travel?

'If you think you can, you can; and if you think you can't, you're right.' Henry Ford

Have you got an answer to the question: *Why Travel?*

"I suppose I should do because everyone else is doing it." *Wrong answer, think again!* Everyone else seems to be buying Sony Playstations and drinking Hooch, but that doesn't mean that you're going to catch me doing it.

Maybe you just want to impress your friends?

Yet again I think that you're barking up the wrong tree here. How impressed will they be if you have a bad time and end up coming back early? Hardly going to be queuing up to buy you a pint now are they! *Think again!*

Going travelling could be an easy excuse for you to get out of something

Running away from a girl/boyfriend, other pressures on you, or maybe you just don't want to be somewhere for the time being. Need I say it... *wrong!* It's not all going to go away just because *you have* for a while.

Factors like boredom, lack of opportunity or dead ends wherever you look may well spur you on to have a desire to travel, but in the end of the day it must be because **you** want to travel. **You** want to see the world. **You** want to see life. **You** want to appreciate life. Maybe you can use it as an opportunity to 'find yourself'.

☞ *Your decision, your life. So do it for yourself, and for no-one else.*

1

The time is right

Every year more and more people of our age are going off travelling around the world... tens of thousands a year. If you think about it you probably know of someone who is doing it at the moment. Therefore if most people know of someone doing it, then can you imagine the amount of backpackers out there? It is easy for me to say it and imagine it, but unless you have seen towns virtually full of backpackers, you can easily be lead to believe that you are going to be on your own out there. **This is simply not the case,** and it's something that I'm going to try and ram home over the course of this book.

☞ With the increase in demand prices are coming down the whole time, so **it's never been cheaper to travel**.

☞ As a result of this massive increase in demand, **it's never been easier to travel.**

Let's take Australia for example

The day you land in Sydney, so will hundreds of others... all about to do the same as you. Buses go up and down the coast from Sydney to Cairns every day. You don't have to lift a finger it's so easy. Get on a bus, and at the next town get off... to be met by representatives from the various hostels with free mini buses. Having spoken to a few people in Sydney, you'll already know which one you want to go to, and so you jump on their bus. When you decide to move on, they take you back to catch the bus, you go to the next town, where it is exactly the same. **It's actually too easy.**

However, it's not just Australia, all over the world there is a well-trodden backpacker trail. Everyone you meet will be on it or will have been on it. Every time you meet up with someone you'll swap a few ideas over a beer or two, and you'll soon know where you should be heading, and what to do when you get there. If you find it too easy, you can make it more difficult for yourself – if not, don't bother! So what are you worried about? "Well now you've mentioned it, Tom, nothing... but no-one's told us this before." Well, it's about time that they did... so now I have. I do appreciate that until you have tried it you are going to be a bit sceptical, so I'm afraid all I can do on this one is say **"trust me!"**

What are you going to come up against?

What do you come up against in life anyway? Highs and lows of course. So why should this be any different?

♦ Challenges

The odd bit of danger and excitement
Real poverty may run up behind you and smack you in the face...
that'll make you think a bit, it did me!
You'll have to live out of your backpack
Look after yourself when you are ill
Face up to every problem and decision that you are going to meet

On the other hand you'll learn

Independence
Self reliance
And the appreciation of people and the things around you.

You are going to learn more about the world, and realise that there is more to life than your local night-club and the odd snog at ten-to-two.

TOP TIP!

Does what I have just said give you a nervous, but exciting buzz? If so, then you are definitely going to have a lot of fun!!

Furthermore, when you come back, you'll be able to answer those questions on TV quiz shows and Trivial Pursuit that leave most people looking as blank as a baffled trout... *so which south-east Asian island does the Equator run through?*

You'll know damn well that it is Sumatra, as you spent four hellish days in the back of a bus trekking up to the bloody thing squashed in between 10 chickens and a goat, the latter of which gave birth, of which too close to comfort experience made you glad that you nicked the sick bag off the plane!

Therefore when it came to that question in Trivial Pursuit, you shout out the answer with glee, and when about to expand on your experience you get cut down by your mate saying "Oh guess what, I bet Tom's bloody been there 'an all", so you pick up the next card and play on! And that is what they call... Life!

Getting back to the working habit

Admittedly it does take a bit of adjusting, but you'll soon get back into it all. The main problem is this great habit whilst travelling of getting up when you like/when the mood takes you. If at this point you decide that you want to stay wherever you are – you stay. If not – you go! It's as simple as that. If you are a naturally free spirited person, then your spirit literally does go free leaving you happy to wander, explore, discover and learn.

Suddenly when you get back to the UK, you may find that everything seems to be moving a lot quicker than you're own relaxed way of life, so quick that you often feel 'spaced' and dizzy for a couple of days when you return. This all depends of course where your last 'port of call' was, whether the urban rush of Los Angeles, or the tropical haven of Thailand. And then you are required, by other people, to be in the office for 9am, have an hour for lunch, and then to finish at 5pm. Or you may be a student, and have to be in a lecture theatre for 10am, have a tutorial at 11am, where you've got deadlines and time schedules to follow. But then we all know that this is the beauty of university, you can take it all in your stride and at your own pace anyway. You can either be an eager busy little bee (like I was at university!), or you can be like a certain housemate of mine who, after 3 years of university, only went to the library once… and that was only to find someone!

Your body has basically been doing this work schedule thing all of its life, and so it won't fail to react to it all again. This is *your* culture, and *your* country. This is what your roots are watered with. Denying it, or using the 'great travelling experience' as a reason for not being able to get back to work I believe is just an excuse for idleness. Theoretically your experience should motivate you to work and do everything that you want to do. It'll all come back to you, so don't worry about it! In relation to what you've just done, it might seem like the worst option, but then this is where your 'itchy feet' come in to the equation. They will help you to dream and relive memories. Every holiday from then on, if you can afford it, you'll be off. You'll certainly enjoy a more active life!

A wasted year?

Don't be ridiculous! Anyone who says that to you has obviously never done anything interesting in their life. How can a year off having fun, exploring amazing countries, broadening your mind, and doing whatever you want to do, be a waste? As far as I'm concerned, a young person sat in an office for a year pushing paper clips around the desk earning money literally to 'piss up the wall'… *is a waste*. No, I'm wrong… it's a *crime!* But that's just my opinion! Why get slated by others because I'm having fun in my life? Jealousy.

I suppose it all depends what you are on this planet for. You only have one chance in life… if you miss the boat – it's gone. *Game Over.*

CHAPTER 2

Decisions

'We pass this way but once. There is no normal, and there's no such thing as normal. There's you, and there's the rest. There's now, and there's forever. Do as you damn well pleasey!' Billy Connolly

The obvious and most important place to start... making decisions! I'm a firm believer in making decisions and sticking to them, only changing them if you really have/want to. With decisions made it is possible to go forward.

Do you know where you want to go?

No? Well I think it's about time you went off to a travel agent to have a little look around! If you've got lots of time before you go, make the most of it and get it all right. So go to the travel agents, pick up a few brochures on a few areas, and have a look at the pictures. Take them home and look at them over the weekend, or over a couple of days. This is actually the best and simplest way. It's true, the brochures will always show the best of the places, but it'll also give you a flavour of what's in store, and definitely start to motivate you. If you're after adventure you'll see photos of rapids, bungy, etc, along with offers and prices for them. You'll be surrounded by pictures of the Inca trails, Australian beaches, the Bush, Ayers Rock, Asian temples, waterfalls, caves, reefs, parrots, mountains, paradise, smiling faces, and young people having fun.

☛ *At this point you'll start to get fairly excited about the prospect of going, which is exactly what you want!*

What next?

After looking through the brochures you'll have some idea about what you want to do, be it visiting just a few countries, loads, Inter-railing, or doing the 'full monty' of some kind of a Round the World trip. Whatever you've decided, you should now take time to actually go and sit down with a travel agent to discuss a proposed trip. Within a day your motivation will be given a huge kick as they will inform you of the relative costs of your trip, whether it is feasible, suggest other ideas/possibilities, and tell you when it is best to go.

TOP TIP!

Ask about the weather cycles of where you want to go, as it may be worth going a month earlier/later so as to miss a monsoon/hurricane season, etc.

There is actually a book out called 'Weather to Travel' (I've put it in the back under '**Some Good Books on the Market**') which is a great book which you can leaf through and work out the best times to be in the countries you want to visit... just 10 minutes of study may be the answer to a really well planned trip. Worth bearing in mind! By the time you eventually walk out the door you will have some definite ideas about **where** *you really* will be going, **when** you may be leaving, and **how much** it is going to cost, as well as a million and one other things buzzing around your head.

Shop around!

Travel agents are usually very obliging, and will help you with your plans. If you do find one that is particularly unhelpful... walk away! There are lots of them around, and you are about to put a lot of money in their pockets, so do shop around. If you think positive and enjoy this first part, we've found that this generally sets you up for the trip. A good place to start could be STA Travel.

Let's get one thing clear, you and me

I know some of you are thinking, 'Hang on a minute, here comes the hard sell from STA Travel!' – **WRONG!**

Let's sort out some ground rules here

Why have I chosen STA Travel?
◆   Simply because I spent time going round all the Thomas Cooks, Lunn Polys, Trailfinders, STA Travel, etc., pretending to be a mystery buyer.
◆   With the response I got I made my decision to go with STA Travel.
◆   I'm not going to bullshit you... why would I want to lose the credibility of what is a good book?

What did I find out?

Well, there seems to be a concentration of cheap student flights towards the student travel market, and the non specialised student travel market can't seem to compete, solely due to the fact that STA Travel can guarantee the airlines loads of customers.

This is my book, and not STA Travel's. It is written by me to give you the best start. I have brought STA Travel into the book simply because I value them to be the best place for you to start. Why?

◆   Low cost fares
◆   Good service – as all their staff are experienced travellers offering first-hand advice
◆   They know what they are doing, having been in the young independent travel business for over 20 years

See for yourself...

Have an idea of where you would like to visit and go to an STA Travel shop, sit down with the staff and have a chat. Ask them all the questions you need to know about itineraries, flights, visas, insurance, prices, etc, and then go elsewhere and see if you can do better. I'd be very surprised if you can! But whatever you do, get some ideas buzzing round in your head so you can make some sort of start. From then on in, it's go, go, go until you take off.

I now want to get you started

Therefore I've asked STA Travel to write a little bit about what's on offer, the possibilities, etc, as they can give you a much more up-to-date/accurate version than anything I can whip up. Use it to shop around if you like, but whatever, I hope for many of you that this will be the first step on the road to the airport and the time of your life. So take it away... STA Travel!

STA TRAVEL

Who are we anyway?
STA Travel are the world leaders in student and young independent travel. With more than 150 branches across Europe, Asia, America and Australia, and over 1,000 well-travelled staff, we have a world of experience to share.

Q. How do I know I'm getting the best prices?
Our prices are competitive, and we use top airlines and tour operators as well as forging cost-effective links with accommodation and car hire specialists. Above all we're set up to deal with the young, independent traveller and can offer you the kind of flexible deals you need... everything from return flights to Europe through to a fully flexible 12 month round-the-world ticket.

Q. How about discounts?
If you're a student or under 26, you can take advantage of lower fares to many destinations. We can issue you with an ISIC (International Student Identity Card) or a Go 25 youth card. Both cost £5 and will entitle you to all kinds of discounts before, during and after your trip.

Q. What happens when I get there?
To make things easier, we can book affordable accommodation in most destinations for the first few nights or longer. We can book you onto organised tours and expeditions, arrange car hire, train and bus passes, internal flights and fully comprehensive insurance. (For more details check our guide

'Groundlevel' or ask at your local STA Travel branch – listed in the back.)

Q. What if I'm not ready to take on the world on my own?

No problem. We can arrange a wide variety of organised tours all over the world, from whirlwind excursions round the sights, to a 36-week overland expedition (see our 'Groundlevel' guide).

Q. What if something goes wrong?

The best part of a journey, the time when you learn the most, can be when things go wrong. But wherever you are in the world, help is at hand from our extensive network of 150 branches, from affiliated Travel Help branches in 77 cities in over 30 countries, or on the phone form our International Helpdesk – you can reverse the charges if neccessary. We also guarantee to refund your ticket in the event of an airline failure. And of course we're ABTA and ATOL bonded.

Q. What if I decide to stay on longer?

You'll almost always get a better deal on fares if you book before you go, but once you've set out, our fares and tickets are very flexible – you can stay in one place longer, leave another place sooner, even change the route with no fuss and little or no cost – this may not seem important now, but it'll mean everything when you've found that perfect beach hut and want to stay there a few weeks longer.

Q. What if I can't get in to a branch to book?

Just call our Telephone Sales department, and they'll be happy to offer advice and make bookings. A low deposit of £50 will secure your seat and full payment guarantees the price of your ticket.

All the clichés are true: travel does broaden the mind, you are only young once, and memories are something that you'll always have, no matter what happens in the future. And with STA Travel's special student and under 26 fares, the trip of a lifetime may never be more affordable… just do it!

Tickets are fully flexible, allowing you really to explore at will. Who knows if you'll want to stay in India for six months, or leave with culture shock after six days? And what if you land at your last destination with only enough cash for a 24-hour spree before flying home? Changing your itinerary as you go along is no problem, and we have over 150 offices across the world to help if you need local advice. The possibilities are limited only by your imagination, and our staff will be happy to help you plan your dream route. Here are just a few of ours:

- London - Los Angeles – Honolulu – Samoa – Aukland – Sydney – Hong Kong – London – *from £698*

- London – Bangkok– Hong Kong – Taipei – Seoul – Los Angeles – Boston – London – *from £703*

- London – Dubai – Calcutta – Singapore – Brunei – Brisbane – Aukland – Los Angeles – *surface* – Miami – Washington – London – *from £836*

- London – Los Angeles – Tahiti – Rartonga – Fiji – Aukland – Sydney – Wellington – Tonga – Honolulu – London – *from £916*

- London – Dubai – Singapore – Brunei – Perth – surface – Melbourne – Aukland – Vancouver – Chicago – London – *from £944*

- London – Los Angeles – Raratonga – Fiji – Auckland – *surface* – Christschurch – Melbourne – Bangkok – London – *from £959*

- London – Prague – Bangkok – surface – Singapore – Tokyo – Honolulu – Boston – London – *from £975*

- Manchester – Bombay – *surface* – Kathmandu – Singapore – Sydney – Wellington – *surface* – Aukland – Raratonga – Los Angeles – New York – Manchester – *from £995*

- London – Johannesburg – Hong Kong – Vancouver – New York – London – *from £1010*

Q. What Insurance should I take?

STA Travel have their own Worldwide insurance which we have developed to suit young independent travellers' needs. We now offer a 'Three Tier' policy with extra cover. We appreciate that you all have different requirements and will require different policies for each trip. Our Budget, Standard and Premier policies provide cover arranged through ISIS.

- The **Budget Policy** is tailormade for backpackers at a very affordable rate.
- The **Standard Policy** provides essential protection at a low price.
- The **Premier Policy** offers more extensive cover and great value for money – particuarly valuable for travel in the USA (due to the expense of their healthcare).

For further details call in to one of our local branches, or get in touch with us (*see* contact numbers at the back).

> *So, as Tom mentioned, feel free to call in at any time to have a chat with our staff. We are there to help, plan trips and realise your dreams. Good luck and have a fantastic trip!*

Just a word from Tom about Round the World packages

For a first time 'Big Trip' these are seen as the best and safest things to buy, and they are perfectly suited to you.

◆ The flights are already booked in advance, so you don't have to worry about organising them.

◆ If you want to stay longer in a country simply ring the airline or contact your travel agent to change the dates of your flights (depending on vadility of ticket and availablility of flights of course).

◆ The only thing you need to remember, which is *fairly* important, is to catch the flight(!). If you don't, your ticket may become invalid and be very difficult to sort out again. You may think that it's odd me mentioning this, but not getting to the airport on time, or just forgetting that you are meant to leave… have happened! The backpackers have then had all sorts of problems.

◆ Also you must remember to confirm your flights 72 hours in advance, as once you are away it is up to you to get in touch with the airline in case the flight times have changed.

◆ Get to the airport two hours before the plane is due to leave. I thought this was solely to do with giving the airline time to get you all on to the plane. However I have been informed that it is in fact policy, and that if you don't turn up on time, they do have the right not to take you (unlikely, but not worth the hassle of testing this theory out!)

Therefore when you hear people talk of Round the World tickets saying that you are tied to flights, limited stays, etc, I'm afraid they're talking bull! Would I lie to you! Furthermore, if there are any financial problems, and say you run out of money on the other side of the world, or if you just want/have to return home for some reason, then you simply change the flights to fly you home as fast as you need to. Simple, eh?

◆ **Build in flexibility**

There is absolutely no point in rushing through fantastic countries just to catch a plane out the other side. You'll end up missing all the good bits, and experience absolutely sod all. When chatting to various foreigners I always hear stories of people visiting only London, and then taking off again with a view that London typifies what England is all about. I can appreciate that a lot of them are simply flying through, and so do not have any more time

11

than a day for a quick 'whip around the capital'. **Have they really seen England?**... 'Why good lord NO old chap!' I can hear a lot of you saying... 'Blighty is more than just the clogged-up streets of Whitehall!' Very true, eh?

So why is it then that hundreds of backpackers every year bugger off thousands of miles around the world to Australia, land in Sydney, get a job, and stay there for 11 months? They then realise at this point what they are actually there for, and so attempt to see Australia in a month, and so fly round quicker than Norman Wisdom on Acid! Is Sydney Australia?? I found that in the end of the day, a city is just a city wherever you are in the world. Yes they all have their attractions and their focal points... but if you go thousands of miles to see a country, you might as well have a look round the friggin thing! By all means come back to Sydney to work, as it is a great place to work to earn money, but don't get stuck there (or anywhere else similar). You might as well be working at home... as you've just jumped from one rat race to another.

Budget for the things that you really do want to do

Cairns, Australia: the home of bungy, rafting, scuba diving, etc, etc. If you are going there for 'adventure', do make sure that you budget your money to do all the things that you want to do. There is nothing worse than getting to a place like this where everyone else is doing all the things that you long to do... except you, because you've basically pissed it all up the wall in big drinking sessions on the way up the coast. So do try and think about these things ahead of time, and budget accordingly.

Finally on the flexibility front, by budgeting, planning and doing everything that you want to do, you should have an absolutely fantastic time. As more and more countries are opening up and becoming more accessible to backpackers than ever before, the packages sold by the travel agents are becoming better and better. *You can now go virtually anywhere you want to... so make sure that you do! Do you have to rush it? No? Didn't think so... so don't!*

So, you think you've found the ideal package?

Before this stage, everything is just talk. As my brother Mat once said, "In this world there are 'doers' and 'talkers'." I'm a 'doer', and the fact that you're reading this means that you are too... so don't blow it at the last minute and become a 'talker'! Once you've bought the ticket therefore you'll find it's plain sailing from here on in. If you need the money, you have to earn it all by this date, and if you're going with a friend, you'll have the added incentive of not letting him or her down. For myself January 7th was the big 'D Day', aged 18. I needed the money and so took every shift possible at McDonalds, and yes... I did leave the country with a spotty face!

TOP TIP!

A good tip here is buy early. By doing this it reduces the option of cancelling (as many have been known to 'bottle it' at the last moment), and you know then that you really are going, as you have a date and time. In fact, once you've paid for it... you're virtually there!

Now you have a date

And I'm not talking about a 'date' with that babe/hunk that you've been eyeing up for ages, even though you 'know their friend', but you still haven't had the courage to go for it. Do it now... great excuse 'Well it's just that I'm going off travelling soon, and I just didn't want to leave without you knowing...!' It worked for me! And anyway, if you get blown out, you'll be on the plane and out of there before you even start to get embarrassed by it! Anyway, back to the plot... *you now have a departure date to aim at.*

From this point you'll be able to organise your time properly

Therefore it's now time to buy essentials like backpacks, sleeping bags, tents, etc... you may even find that your birthday, Christmas, or even both fall in between the time you buy your ticket and go. So why not surprise those caring relatives of yours by actually asking for something useful for your travels... and not another pair of socks that you're never going to wear and that are going to go at the back of the drawer! Little things such as a small torch, penknife, travel saucepan, etc. (*see* **Packing**) which you will find invaluable, but which added expense you could do without.

Your 'Rellies' will then think that they are helping you on your way, and you in turn can allow them to believe that they have performed this wondrous deed by mentioning in their postcard about how you're finding it odd *not wearing any socks* out in Peru, but how the mini torch they gave you saved you (and your friends) from imminent danger when you got lost in some caves in the mountains... when in fact you'll probably find it invaluable helping everyone find their way back to the hostel after a great night out, or for seeing turtles hatching on the beach, or something as mundane or trivial like that!

What do I see as the key?

Well I'm sure you know by now what I'm going to say! Time for another...

TOPTIP!

Be positive and book early... buy the ticket and think about where you are going, what you are doing, how you will afford it, what your budget is, and how you are going to plan it all.

You'll suddenly find that you'll take more of an interest in the holiday programmes on TV, travel supplements in the paper, and novels on people's travelling experiences, etc. 'I'm off there!', 'That's where I'm going!'... but be careful not to drive too many people nuts! Unfortunately you'll come up against a lot of jealousy, but don't let it put you off. If they wanted to do it they would have done it already. They're 'talkers' and just don't like seeing others have the guts to do something they'd never have the nerve to do themselves... you're doing it, so good for you!

However just general 'chatter' about your impending trip will really excite you even more about the whole thing. But at the same time you will be nervous, of course you will, you'd be daft to deny it. Before the Canadian trip, due to lack of money/idea about what I was about to do, I was nervous right up to the departure... although I tried to let my friends see that I wasn't (male macho image, or something like that!) But once you are on your way, on the plane, boat, or in the car, a real sense of adventure and nervous excitement takes over... you're off, and there's no going back! This is of course totally untrue, as if ever you don't enjoy it (unlikely) or feel you've had enough for whatever reason... you can easily come home. There is no shame in doing that, at least you've given it a go.

☛ *If you are your own person, then you can go wherever, or do what ever you want... can't you?*

What did we use for motivation?

Why do you want to know this? Well, maybe you would like to equate with us, and see how much in the same situation you are with a lot of other people at the moment. Last week I read an article in *The Times* about how 'year out' people are on the increase. There seems to be less out there for people our age at the moment, and so a year out travelling the world just seems like a great viable alternative at the moment.

- Well... **boredom** was actually the biggest factor amongst us all. Colin for example was on the dole before he left... unmotivated and in need of a change, and desperate to get out of England for a while. 'It just seemed like a good idea at the time!'
- Have you been studying 'hard' for a few years? (or maybe I should just say have you been studying!).
- Always doing the same thing, always going to the same places... seeing the same people, talking about the same thing?
- Or maybe you've been in a job where you're now at a point where the novelty has worn off, you always seem to be working, everything is the same, and you seem to have dropped into a 'live to work, work to live' routine.

- *You're young... you have the chance to break from this... so do it before it's too late.*

Take hold of your life... now!

Whenever I've said something along these lines about getting bogged down in work to others, the reaction always seems to be *'well that's life, Tom!'*... usually said to me by older generations. However things have changed since their day, and I'm sorry *but that is not life!* Fifteen years ago it was fairly uncommon for people our age to take time out and travel the world, these were experiences only had by those in the armed forces who had to serve overseas, or people in shipping, foreign office, etc. The 'normal routine' therefore was (and still is if you think about it) to get qualifications, get a job, settle down, and then do your travelling over a long period of time in a series of two week holidays, where you often get to see nothing more than the hotel, the pool, and a few restaurants and beaches... *might as well stay at home!* Once you hit the late 20s and above you start to have commitments, you can't just up and leave with only a moments notice. This is why so many of the people that I've met on my travels have encouraged me, always saying about how they missed out when they were young.

So don't miss out, life is what you make of it. You're going to have plenty of years to settle down to a job, enter the 'rat race', etc. One year in your life of having fun and doing everything that you want is only going to benefit you (as I've said before... what is the difference between working for 43 years and 44 years?... Isn't it great being able to look at things from a different angle)... *so GO!*

Additional planning tips

Other motivators?... well everything from

♦ adventure
♦ adrenalin
♦ curiosity
♦ 'discovering yourself', and putting things in perspective
♦ Even a little bit of **research into the countries** you are about to visit, i.e. their capitals, the seasons, temperatures, what they produce, etc.
♦ If you find it interesting you could even check up on the **political situation** at the time will things be changing while you are there?
♦ There may also be **major events** happening around the time that you are there, which you may be able to coincide with your visit e.g. South East Asian Olympics, elections, Australia Day, Independence Day, national festivals, etc. (*see* appendix '**World-wide Events**' at the back of the book).

All of this tends to help build the excitement, makes your trip more eventful, and even helps to give you a broader knowledge and an understanding of events that are happening on the other side of the world. In Tony's own words:

☞ *'You've got to remember that the rest of the world has far more to offer than what can be found on your doorstep'... something that I think that a lot of us tend to forget, as we get absorbed into our own little worlds and everything that revolves just around us.*

Did I hear someone say 'rat race'?

CHAPTER 3

Packing

English Proverb (late 16th century) "A traveller must have a falcon's eye, an ass's ear, an ape's face, a merchant's words, a camel's back, a hog's mouth, and a stag's legs."
...a fair description of one of my drunken snogs!

Do you really need it?

Another essential chapter, but again mostly common sense. Picture the scenario, a friend of mine Tim, off to Australia... does he really need to take his favourite new pair of Cat boots? Of course I knew that he wanted to impress the ladies, but weighing about a kilo, it's a lot to take in your backpack (as well as the bulkiness of them). If you are going to hot countries think hot! Indeed there may well be times when you want to go hiking (Tim's excuse), but you will invariably find that you will be able to hire these things on site, or that a multi-purpose pair of strong trainers may do the trick... you'll find everyone's a bit less fashion conscious when they're travelling. In fact Tony, possibly one of the vainest people this side of the Equator, was even known to wear a cagoule when the rain came down, although I was sworn to secrecy at the time!. DOH!... secret's out!

What is a good backpack?

Our important tip is to **PACK LIGHT, leave home with a half empty backpack** if possible... because by the time you return it will be weighing 10 times the original weight and bursting at the seams with all the 'bits and pieces' that you've acquired along the way. This is why it really is essential to **buy yourself a decent backpack** if you don't already have one. With the amount of travelling, carrying and general 'lumping around' that you will be doing, a comfortable backpack is essential. You've got to remember that this will be your personal 'caravan' for a long period, and if it falls apart (like mine did in Canada) it will cause you nothing but unnecessary aggro all the way round. 65 litres is usually sufficient, with some of the 'petite' amongst us opting for the 55 litre. (Test the Exodus 65 v Exodus 55 by Vango).

◆ If, like me initially, you've never carried or packed a backpack before, do go to a camping shop and ask for their own personal advise. This proved invaluable to me. When my backpack did start to get heavy, of being a relatively small stature (but great personality!), I didn't break my back.

◆ With this book there is a Millets Discount. There is a store near you, and they have a huge range of back packs, sleeping bags, tents, etc. So take the book and get your discount (ace pack = Eurohike Traveller 65).

◆ When you're in the shop, make sure you have time to spend a bit of time there. Talk to the assistants about any questions/concerns that you have; after all, that's what they are there for.

◆ If they aren't being helpful, get the manager to explain it all. If the manager isn't helpful, hint that you're not going to spend fifty-odd quid on the wrong back pack, and then threaten to get Head Office to put a rocket up their arse... should get some co-operation!

◆ When in the shop why not get some things to put in to the back to see how heavy it is.

TOP TIP!

Some questions you might like to think about:
◆ Is it comfortable? ◆ Can I adjust it? ◆ How do I
adjust it? ◆ How am I meant to pack it? – weight at the
top/bottom? – where should my sleeping bag go? (to be
accessed daily) ◆ Does it have reinforcers to stop it bulging
when it gets full? ◆ Could it possibly leak? – should I seal it?
◆ Can I make the bag secure? – can the zips be padlocked
together? – are the holes in the zips wide enough for the pad-
lock to go through? ◆ Why is this model cheaper than the
rest? (if word 'quality' appears in the answer... beware!)
◆ I have a bad back/damaged shoulder/pregnant/three arms –
which one is best suited to me?

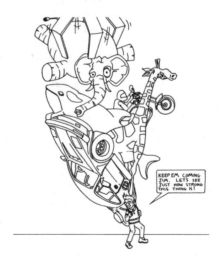

KEEP EM COMING
JIM. LET'S SEE
JUST HOW STRONG
THIS THING IS!

☞ *YOU'VE GOTTA GET A GOOD ONE. I can't hammer this point*
home enough. You are a 'backpacker' after all... .your job is to have
a pack – on your back! Nuff said.

There is a voucher in the back of this book to help you get started in buying backpacks, sleeping bags, etc... it'll save you a fair bit of money... so do
use it.

What to take?

Well... I did a little survey of my group of contributors, and it was amazing how most of us came up with the same things. But when you think about it, it's not too surprising, as we now all know to keep it light and pack only the bare essentials. The following is therefore an idea of some of our contents to give you an idea of what you may be forgetting, and also to make you think whether you do need to take that 'Best of Eric Clapton' CD on the off chance that you may find a CD player somewhere in Nepal so that you can listen to Layla because it will remind you of a class night with your best friend two summers ago! There are also a few other 'bits and bobs' you may think are a good idea to take:

ESSENTIAL...

Backpack	Toilet paper (flat pack)
Candles	Penknife + attachments
Small torch	Sunglasses – cheap ones!
Address book + pens	Camera + film
Pack of tissues	Knife/fork/spoon set
Matches/lighter	Sewing kit
Light clothes line	Small hairbrush/comb
Alarm clock	Universal sink plug (useful)
Small purse/wallet	Pack of cards

Padlocks (+ chain?) for backpack
- makes you feel more confident about leaving your bag, and are fairly essential when you think there are thieves about.
- don't want the hassle of keys? Get a combination one.

Plastic bags
- small ones with a seal... you'll be amazed how often they come in handy, especially keeping things dry, or preventing wet/leaky things wetting everything else.
- shopping ones e.g. Tesco... you'll find that it takes a long time to get things dry, so these are ideal to put wet things in, and for separating your items in your backpack.

Sleeping bag
- check for climate that you are going to and what 'season' bag you'll need, some hot countries get very cold at night... as Colin found to his peril in Zimbabwe. Be safe – get a warm one.

Sleeping sheet
- often required in hostels so get one!

Synthetic drawstring bags
- again ideal for dirty washing and as a separate bag for everyday use.

Towels

◆ main one shouldn't be too big or too thick. Remember that you are going to have problems getting it dry, so air/wash it as often as possible to stop smelling.

◆ often a good idea to take a small hand towel as well. This can be carried in your day bag and will come in handy for a lot of things... as a pillow/head rest, for drying yourself when your backpack isn't around, etc.

Travel saucepan

◆ small, closes shut so you can store things in it when you travel, and perfect size for whipping up a meal for yourself... eat out of it and save on washing up!

Travel wash

◆ fantastic little item as can wash clothes in hot or cold water.

Washbag

◆ full of usual rubbish, I'm sure I don't have to remind you to take your toothbrush. However things like tweezers, small pair of scissors (usually in First Aid Kit), small scrubbing brush, and best of all... nail clippers can be invaluable.

◆ For example nail clippers to me are vital, they always have been. Use to cut everything apart from nails!... remove objects from feet/body that shouldn't be there, cutting things – basically I reckon I could perform a minor heart operation with them if the need arose. Invaluable!

VITAL

Contact Lenses

◆ make sure that you have enough solution, protein tablets, etc.

◆ also worth having a pair of glasses as well (can be made up dead cheaply now, so not as expensive as you may think) as there may be times when it is impossible to wear lenses.

Condoms

◆ condoms are free at Family Planning, if not they are available at all chemists and even at some petrol stations now (they'll soon be free with every £20 of unleaded no doubt!)

◆ should be carried now by both men and women as it is the 'responsible thing to do', someone else may need them even if you don't at that moment.

Drivers licence

◆ home + international – again, make sure it has the correct address on it.

E111

♦ your health document, essential if in Europe, may be useful elsewhere.

Finances

♦ Money
♦ Travellers Cheques – *see* Finances
♦ Credit cards

ID Cards

♦ always extremely useful.
♦ If you are a student make sure you carry an ISIC card as proof of student ID, as in many places it may entitle you to discounts… always worth asking everywhere! However, with the amount of fakes on the market (can be bought out in Thailand for about £5, bought by people under the age of 21 so they can drink in America… allegedly… of course I don't know anything about this!), it is worth taking some extra ID to back up your claim, as some people have been known to turn the ISIC card down.
♦ Other ID, such as a 'Proof of Age Card' or a photocopy of your birth certificate, are other essentials, as they always make any checks or paperwork go a lot quicker.

Passport!

♦ you'd be surprised how many people forget! Make sure it is valid for the whole period you are away, and that you have all the necessary visas, or you're going to have serious problems later on - see **'Tips and Hints'** also.

☞ *NB ensure it is signed and has the correct address on it.*

Do you have dual nationality?

♦ If yes, then you are an extremely lucky bugger, as you may be able to avoid queues, and be able to work in countries where many others can't. It is advisable therefore to get them both up to date, and use the full benefit of them.

Passport photos

♦ worth having a few with you kept in a nice dry place, often needed for temporary visas, permits, ID cards, etc.

Photocopies

♦ of all essential documents. You may even like to give some copies to your parents, i.e. of passport, air tickets, insurance documents, credit cards and emergency numbers, travellers cheques numbers, etc.

◆   important to keep separate copies in your backpack and day bag, so if one gets lost, you're all right Jack!

◆   medical: important to have copies of your GP's address, your medical insurance documents, evidence of jabs, blood group, allergies, etc. Especially if allergic to something like Penecillin **+ let others you travel with know.**

References

◆   of work experience. Especially useful for bar work, silver service waiting etc. It is also a good idea to take evidence of qualifications such as GCSE's, 'A' levels, Degree and anything else you think may be of interest.

Sanitary towels

◆   unfortunately for the girls these are not free at the family planning, and it is wise to stock up. As mentioned in the section on **Female Solo**, it is available just about everywhere, although it won't be the slim comfortable stuff that you are usually using… bulky, but it does the job!

Suncream + sunblock

◆   I took sun factor 6, because I am usually used to wearing 4 maximum, 2 or tanning oil (as I have fairly olive skin). Unfortunately in Fiji the sun was a LOT hotter than I was used to, and so I fried really badly… something to do with the Ozone layer I think! So be prepared. You'll tan just as well with a 15, and besides you've got plenty of time to get a tan if you want one. It's no longer a quick 2 weeks in the Costa del Sol with the family or the lads/lassies beano to Mallorca, although you'll find the excitement and heat of both up the east coast of Australia, and in the backpacker havens of Thailand!

◆   Boots have a Sun Shop Consultant now in all of their major stores, so make sure that you go in and ask their advice if you are unsure.

'AIDS kit'

◆   again essential, is a sterilised pack that contains needles, etc., that can be given to a doctor in the event of an emergency wherever you are.

First Aid Kit

◆   essential, make sure it is full of things you need, ie. plasters, sterilised bits and pieces… the ones you can buy in the shops are pretty good (e.g. Boots).

Evidence of injections

◆   always advisable to keep in a safe place.

These last 3 should be kept in an easily accessible place so they can be whipped out in an emergency, both for yourself, but also for other people.

TOP TIP!

'The Runs', 'Galloping Trots', 'Squits', or more politely... 'Traveller's Tummy'. Lomotil or Diafed do the business better than an Albanian shot putter with an industrial mallet and a cork! Take them with you in your First Aid kit, but be wary about letting some of the infection out before plugging it up, as it can be very dangerous. Remember to re-hydrate – 'Rehydrate' or flat Coke drunk slowly does the job perfectly.

DAY BAG

This is so much of an essential item that it warrants a paragraph of its own. It is advised to have a day bag for a number of reasons.

♦ By getting one that you can padlock, or secure in some way, you can use it as your own personal 'safe' and keep all your most important items in it, such as your passport, money, tickets, documents, etc. I find that it's useful to put all of these inside a money belt inside the bag.

♦ You'll find that with all these things in one small bag that you'll never let it out of your sight, and you'll get used to always putting it in secure places wherever you end up, so you'll always have peace of mind.

♦ The day bag is also useful for the travelling part of the trip. If you have a small towel in there you can use it for washing, or for a cushion on those all too long and tedious bus/train rides. If you are in the airport and the plane is delayed and your luggage has gone through, it can be a life saver to have things like a washbag, books, food, cards, spare undies, etc., with you.

What sort of bag?

♦ Well many like to take one of those little backpacks as they're nice and comfortable to carry. Many backpacks now have these attached 'all-in-one'.

♦ However if it is a 65 litre backpack with one of these bags on the back, e.g. the Eurohike Traveller 65 at Millets, do have a think, because this will reduce the 'main backpack' to about a 55 litre capacity, as the day pack makes up the other 10 litres of the 65 litres. Will this be too small?

♦ The other option is a small holdall which can be collapsed and zipped up flat into virtually nothing.
Either of these are ideal as they can easily be put away into your backpack or attached back on to your backpack when not needed.

OPTIONAL

Address cards
◆   handy if your bag gets lost, means it will eventually come back to you!
◆   get some personalised ones made up, great to swap (but easy to lose).

Battery shaver
◆   how hairy are you? Sometimes they work for you, others have to be content with disposables… if so take enough if not visiting a developed country for a while. Or maybe you're looking forward to cultivating that long awaited beard?… chance to do it!

Black marker pen
◆   you'd be surprised where this comes in useful. Things like marking food bags when you put them in the communal fridges, essential for hitch hiking, and generally for marking anything else that I can't think of right now. I love them… but then I have always been a bit odd!

BT Chargecard
◆   great way of being able to afford to stay in touch with relatives. Can be 'made to measure' in that it can be only used to dial certain numbers. Your parents will take care of the bill, and so can keep track of the expense. Lines like 'well… at least I wouldn't have an excuse not to get in touch… there are phones all over the world nowadays' seem to work well if you want to get one.
◆   Highlight the fact that it can only be used to ring their number so that it will put their mind at ease (no worries about someone nicking it and running up huge bills at your parents' expense!)

Diary
◆   even I've kept diaries of my travels! Great to read later on, but also help to remember names of places and friends for future reference.

Inflatable neck pillow
◆   if you've got one and find it comfortable to use, why not take it? It packs away to nothing, and I'm sure you'll find it dead useful on those long journeys.

Mosquito net
◆   if travelling to really hot countries where it's required

Multi Vitamins
◆   worth getting a batch of them to supplement your diet, especially in areas where your eating habits may change/be a bit dodgy (ie. it really is a 'Hot Dog'!)

Personal Alarm

see '**Tips**' *Protection*.

Poncho

again can be a great asset to cover yourself + bag from heavy rain.

Roll mat

essential if taking a tent as you'll find the ground very hard; also very handy for sitting on when waiting for buses, on beaches, etc.

Tent

if travelling solo or with a friend can turn out to be a lot cheaper to live in (*see* **Hints**)

Tubigrip

you know, the stuff you can put on most parts of your body when you have an injury. A girl in Australia once showed me how she wears it at the top of her thigh under her shorts as a way of concealing her money. As it is tight you can hide notes in it safely. It was such a good idea that I asked her to show me it again later (after I had had a few beers)... unfortunately all I got was a slap!

Walkman + tapes

good idea to have for those long journeys that you may be going on. However the downside is things like having to look after it (damp/being knocked around/damage), and if it is a nice one... 'making sure that it doesn't walk man!' (bad joke, but I really don't care!), making sure that no-one nicks it.

but are quite a good idea, and great for letting other people listen to what sort of music we have over here, and vice-versa... conversational pieces!

Waterproof pouch

I was given one of these at Christmas. Possibly a good idea in hot countries to stop sweat moulding your money, travellers cheques, and passport. If you feel insecure at any time, you can always take them into the shower/sea with you.

It is also a good idea if you are going trekking, as it will keep all the important things dry. I'm certainly going to use it next time, so I'll let you draw your own conclusions. I'll let you know how I get on with it once I've used it!

Water purification tablets

taste like an old pair of manky pants, but then at least you know that the water is safe. I had some once, never used them, but kept them because I was fascinated by the way they became mouldy... loads of lovely colours!

◆ do you need them? Depends on where you are going of course. If you think that you do, get 'em.

◆ however you can buy bottled water just about anywhere now. The European stuff is usually safer than the 'Eau de Local Piss', but do watch for 'tampering'. If the seal on the top is damaged, or looks as fake as a political manifesto... leave well alone, OR buy it, drink it, and then sit on the toilet for the next three days finding out what it is like to shit acid!

CLOTHES

TOP TIP!

Think light, loose fitting cotton... as they dry out quickly and are not too hot.

Hat

◆ beware of sun stroke!... when going into the southern hemisphere or near the equator many (like myself) don't realise how hot the sun really is. I'll tell you now... it really does do your head in, making you feel rotten, nauseous, and not at all well... not what you want when everyone else is at the local bar enjoying themselves.

◆ also necessary to cover up in some countries if entering sacred buildings, etc... especially with the ladies, usually best to ask; remember, they're not bothered about fashion either!

Sarongs

◆ for men and women... no lads, it's not just a skirt! Sarongs are great, and in my eyes essential for backpacking, as they double as sheets, wraps, towels, shawls, beach towel, but also necessary to wear over your legs when entering sacred buildings in many countries.

Shirt

◆ again light material, plus long sleeved. This stops you being eaten alive by insects, and in the event of sunburn will keep you covered up and not irritate the area too much.

Shoes

◆ always the big problem. I've always found light trainers to be the best, as if you're walking around a lot in hot countries you'll find 'heavy' trainers sweat profusely and so smell quite badly. If like me you have a problem with smelly feet... beware! Whatever you do make sure you break them in and that you air your shoes as much as possible. The odd wash now and again won't go amiss either. If you're not sure go into a shoe shop and ask their advice about what's best.

◆ be aware that you might wear them whilst walking in the sea or in wet 'jungly' conditions (or something like that). The point here is that if your trainers have that **leather stuff on top**... you're buggered! If you've had them before you know how after a fair bit of 'wear and tear' the leather rots/breaks up. Well, wearing them the whole time will lead to them disintegrating very quickly. **'Synthetic' is the name of the game here.**

◆ a lot of people end up wearing thongs (or 'flip flops' as we say in the UK!) which no longer have an un-trendy image when you travel as they really are the most practical things to wear! They're great for temples, hot places, showers (to avoid veruhcas, etc), going to the beach, etc.

Shorts/Skirts

◆ if in hot countries you'll be in them all the time, so get a few pairs of a tough material.

◆ men can get away very well with swimming shorts if you're going to spend a bit of time on beaches, swimming, etc.

◆ and for the girls, the short wrap around skirts/sarong are ideal for covering a swimming cossie, or just for everyday wear in hot countries.

Smart clothes

◆ you may like to carry a set of 'smart clothes' with you for possible job interviews, working in, or for going out to smart places. I usually take a smart pair of low cut shoes (i.e. not ankle high) that can be shined up, a good pair of trousers, a good shirt, and a tie. All these can be used for other purposes, and are invaluable (so you'll be glad that you took them) when you need them.

Thermals

◆ if going to cold countries, or even hot countries that may be very cold at night, thermals are great... don't be shy, be warm. So take those Long Johns and wear them with pride! On the odd really cold day when I was a student in Manchester I used to wear them (leftovers from the trip to Russia)... lovely and warm... didn't tell anyone though, until now that is. DOH!

T Shirts/light tops

◆ a few are a good idea as you will find yourself always wearing and washing these.

- in hot countries you will obviously sweat more, so if you take old ones away with you you might find them falling apart fairly soon, so try to take ones with strong stitching on the shoulders for example.
- T Shirts with prints on them can be very useful to take as they are good for 'conversation starters'. Wearing a bungy T shirt, or one with something about England, windsurfing, football have lead to people coming up to me and starting a conversation. If you have something with your home town/school/university on you will soon meet people and find out what a small world it is after all!

Trousers/jeans

- beware if taking jeans: if hot, can be too hot… if get wet, take ages to dry and can make you very cold… if trekking **don't** wear them because if they do get wet they can lead to hypothermia. They are bulky, but are handy to go out at night.
- light material trousers are best, as are cool and not bulky to pack.

Underwear

- as much as you think necessary, but again easy to wash and quick to dry.

Warm sweat-shirt

- of some kind… heavy + bulky, so keep to bare minimum.

TOP TIP!

If one of your first stopping off points is a country like America or Asia where clothes are a lot cheaper than over here, why not save some money and wait until you get there to buy your clothes? However, if you are a terrible shopper, and the sight of all those cheap clothes would just make you flip out, and spend, spend, spend, …buy at home, as backpackers have been known accidentally to spend most of their money at the first stop, fill their packs with unwanted junk, and suffer for the rest of the trip. You can also budget better by buying everything before you go and then forcing yourself to buy only necessary items… a safer idea when you're on a tight budget.

NB You may well experience weight change... even Tony lost some weight, although you wouldn't think it to see him now (it's not a belly, it's a generator for a sex machine!). So do think about loose fitting clothes. They'll not only be more comfortable for when you are travelling around, but more practical, as with drawstring/elastic at the top, they'll always be OK if the pounds come on/off. Fashion? Remember that it doesn't count when you travel, so be practical.

OTHER POSSIBLE

Balloons/pens
you'll meet a lot of 'fascinated' kids on the way, it's always nice to give them little presents like this that they'll really like.

Books
heavy/bulky to carry, but easy to swap with other backpackers. In a lot of hostels you will find a book swapping shelf where you can swap your books for free.

Map of world
always good to have one, so at least you know generally where you are and where you're going. Good as a visual aid when getting tips on places. Apparently you can 'borrow' them from the airline magazines, but again I wouldn't know anything about this terrible practice. On the other hand, the magazines are just thrown away when they are out of date, so why not put parts of it to good use?

Marmite
it is good for you, lasts for ages and makes a great snack with a loaf of bread (just make sure it is stored in an unbreakable place, or you'll have that lovely Marmitey smell following you everywhere!)

Photos of family
so you know why you left home for 8 months! Also makes you a 'real' person (i.e. not just a 'travel bum') if you have problems with officials.

☞ PACKING?... THE RULES ARE SIMPLE:
If you can't afford to lose it
If you don't think you need it
If you can buy it cheaper overseas
If it's bigger than your backpack
If it weighs more than you

DON'T TAKE IT!

Parents

CHAPTER 4

'Travel, in the younger sort, is a part of education: in the elder, a part of experience.' Francis Bacon.

When talking (often... too often maybe!) about writing this book, the subject of parents always invariably arose. As I bore people to sleep with tales of Scuba Diving on the Great Barrier Reef, Sky Diving in Canada, the beaches of Thailand, and the arrogance of Americans (not all, just a few!), many parents ask 'Would you send your own son/daughter off round the world?' To this I have no real answer, as at 22 the thought of having children sounds as appetising as a naked roll in the snow with David Mellor! I would of course say '**YES!**', as the education, experience, and maturity that they will gain will be invaluable in life. When the time comes that I will buy a pair of slippers and a pipe, settle down, have kids, allow them to grow up, and then approach the age of 18, I will actively encourage them to travel and broaden their horizons.

The problems of letting go

Many parents remark that their children certainly do change when they travel, many 'for the better' (as in the poem in the front of my book). But it is easy to forget that at the age of 18+, we are in fact adults. Of course everyone is different. Some families actively encourage their children to move away, 'grow up', and find their feet in life. Others however find it difficult to let go, they stay very protective, maybe not being able to come to terms with the fact that their children have grown up. I'm not sure if it is a feeling of all those years put into a child's life, the shaping, the expense, the good and the bad times, or just the feeling of being in control, and not wanting to lose that control. At the end of the day, you are their children, and it is often difficult for them to let you go off and do something which they may see as dangerous. It's your job to make them see that it isn't as dangerous as they think, and that you're doing it for your own good.

Everyone is so different in what they believe in, and what they do. This is what I find very interesting, and yet very difficult about this subject. For instance I know that a lot of parents will read this section of the book. Although they like to sit back and watch what you do from a distance, the interest is always there. From the conclusions that have been drawn from my contributors to this book, many have witnessed their parents reading up on places, reading the Lonely Planet guides, and trying to help out as much as possible. Others have seen a total disinterest until just before take off, or until they actually return.

Parents will worry, because it is their job to worry!

The point is that this section is going to be an absolute nightmare to write, but I think that it is one of the most important chapters in the book. There are always a lot of things that we always want to say to each other, but never come out. There are a lot of things that your parents would like you to know, but won't say... like the fact that they do care a helluva lot about you, and that if you don't get in contact for a couple of months, they *will* worry about you! You may think that when you go out at night and say that you will be back very late, that they won't particularly care. However many won't sleep easy until they know that you are safely home. So your decision to go off travelling around the world won't simply be taken with a pinch of salt!

So what do I hope to achieve in this chapter?

Well, just to bring up a few issues.

◆   I feel that good communication on the subject is always best before you go
◆   Once you've gone, they want to know what you are up to
◆   Roughly where you are
◆   And a rough idea of what your plans are

Apparently there is nothing worse than your parents answering questions about you starting with the words 'I really don't know... ', 'He/She never told me... 'or, 'Well I haven't heard for a while, but I'm assuming that he/she is all right!' So get the communicating part right from the start after you have made the decision to go.

Learn from my mistakes!

For me this is a very personal wish. I had opposition from my dad all the way. His refusal to accept that I was finally reaching adulthood, turned my year out before University into a real struggle. It made me resent him, and made it very difficult to sort myself out before I left. By the time that I left I couldn't wait to get away. This is how it **shouldn't** be, and so I hope that I am in a great position to make sure others learn from my mistakes.

Looking back on it now, **that I persevered and fought for my dream of going of travelling around the world was the best move I ever made** Why? Because my dad thought that he knew what was best *for me*. He wouldn't accept that possibly I knew what I wanted to do, and that I was in charge of my own life. Unfortunately there is an acceptance in this world that everyone should do what is socially acceptable, and what is the norm. In our family, everyone has gone to school, got their exams, got into university, and got jobs. Work, work, work, and then die. Doesn't that sound morbid! But true. It always seems to me that there is this unwritten law which says that you should do this, and any break from this is frowned upon. Well frown upon me then! I did it, and I'm glad that I did it!

I think it is more to do with the fact that the people who are frowning upon you are those ones who haven't done all that they would have liked with their lives, and who are jealous of you for breaking from the norm and doing something exciting. Many parents who haven't travelled may see it as nothing more than a glorified holiday, and will refuse to see any benefits that you could get from it at all. Those that have, like Tony's dad (who was in the merchant navy), believe that their children should see the world as they did.

☛ *But in the end of the day, it's what you get out of it, and no-one else.*

Grab hold of your own life!

I suffer constant jibes about "it's about time you got a job". Why? I don't feel that I'm ready just yet to jump on the long 43 year slog to my retirement! Yes, I will get down to getting a job soon. In fact at the moment I am filling in application forms for various Grauate Student Schemes here and there.

So while you have the chance, grab hold of your own life for a change, and don't let others make these decisions for you. You're not a sheep are you? So don't follow others around!

Many will say that you are wasting a year in life

Bull, you are gaining a year of incredible worldly experince. The difference between working 43 years and 44 years! Ridiculous eh? Don't let your parents hold you back because they haven't been able to do what you are doing (they forget that it was actually different in their day), or because they think it is about time that you went to college/got a job. If you have to struggle for it, then Good Luck, I know how difficult it is going to be for you. But if it can be any other way, then do it. Don't end up resenting your parents, as in the end of the day they are only looking out for our best interests.

That's the ironic thing, you are both struggling to look after your own interests.

The only answer is "Well, who rules your life then?" I'm sure that if you show them that you want to be in control of your own life, and do what you want to do… in a sane manner of course!… then they will be proud of you, and give you all the help possible. Try and make them see it from your point of view. They will eventually become resigned to the fact that you are off and so come round in the end. In the end of the day, they probably won't want to alienate you, as much as you don't want to alienate them.

Reassurance

◆ That you will be all right
◆ That you will be sensible at all times
◆ And that you'll ring/write home on a regular basis
◆ And at times of need – *don't be proud!*

◆ **Mums will tend to worry about 'mumish' things,** i.e. will you eat properly, get a horrible disease, mugged, etc.
◆ **Dads tend to worry about the financial side,** i.e. organising your finances, being left with large credit card bills/letters blackmailing him for more money… combined with your mum nagging him about leaving you to starve on the other side of the world!
◆ **Dads will also worry about mumish things, but after years of leaving it up to your mum, will continue to do so here!**

TOP TIP!

Can you cook? Why not get a crash course off your mum or dad? It's something that you can prac-tise every day before you leave. It will further reassure your parents that you will in fact feed yourself while you're away. It is also a lot cheaper, and better for you, than that 'Wopper McDogburger' at the local take-away!

This is all unavoidable, but quite nice in a way, because you realise that despite everything you thought in your teen years, they are not out to get you, and that they really do care!

Support and advice from your planning stages right up to your leaving will always be appreciated, and is the best start to your trip. If they want to get involved, let them! Who else will persuade those distant relatives to give you useful presents for your travels for Christmas? Who else will remind you about your doctor's appointments, or give you valuable tips about packing.

Keep your parents informed

♦   When you have made that decision to travel and actually have a route booked and sorted out, keep your parents 'in the know'.

♦   Give them a general outline of what the route is, and make them aware (and of course be aware yourself!) that the route might actually change.

♦   And if you find that the route does actually change for whatever circumstances, say that you will inform them… and make sure you do, they'll thank you for it!

TOP TIP!

Never, on any account, go off round the world without letting your parents know. 'Yeah hi mum, no I'm not at Jason's, I'm in Bangkok. What do you mean 'When am I coming home?' I don't know, in a year or so, a bit longer maybe? Sorry… what exactly do you mean about Dad setting fire to my bedroom…! …It won't be appreciated!

There have been a couple of times when I have literally gone walkabout and my parents didn't really know where I was. I didn't really care at the time because I was having a great laugh and so didn't really think about anybody else. In fact there was a time on my first trip when I didn't speak to my parents for a fair while, and then I rang up (feeling a bit low and sorry for myself) having just had a ceiling fan extracted from my head! All I wanted was a bit of sympathy… but looking back on it now it wasn't the best thing I'd ever done, not getting in touch for a while and then ringing up because I had damaged myself. I guess they started to believe that I would only ring if I was in trouble or something.

This was a habit I got out of pretty damn quick after I got a major bollocking off a 'mother' that I met whilst diving on the Barrier Reef up in

Cairns. I reckon this woman went round making backpackers feel guilty for a living. However... the message got across and it hit home hard.

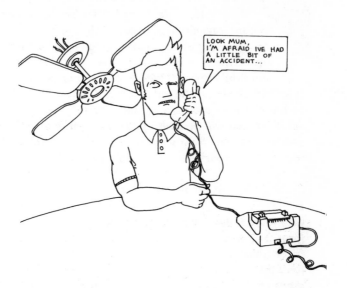

KEEPING IN TOUCH

Bingo! Think I've hit the big one here! From what I've just said above I think you'll gather how important I think this is. **Sort this one out between you before you go, and you'll all be a lot happier.** There are a few alternatives to choose from, so think about them and come to a few decisions before leaving, rather than getting on the plane throwing a few half-hearted promises around.

Your parents don't want to know that when you get bored one day, and have nothing else to do, that you'll send them a scatty postcard, indicating nothing more than the rough area of the world that you are in, the fact that at the time of writing you obviously had some sort of health (and a limb to write with), and that you couldn't care less if they hear from you at all. What they want to hear is that you will write from every country, so that they can map your progress, or ring on 'Days' that you can't possibly forget, such as your birthday, Cup Final day, etc.! It's not only for their benefit, it might be for you as well. What if they need to get in touch with you for some important reason? Something you would like to know? This pact, and trust that you will actually keep in touch, really does help a lot.

BIG TIP TIME!

As with any of the methods I am about to talk about, please don't make it a 'regular' thing. By all means regular in the sense that you will ring/write every once in a while… to be agreed by you. But not every Sunday, or the first Monday of the month at 6pm, or anything like that. Why not? Well because your parents will have it written down on the calendar, and may well look forward to the call with a big list of things to tell you, news, friends, etc. Each call will be built up, by telling friends/relatives that they are to hear from you on that day, and that they will in turn recount your news in the days following.

Meanwhile… At 6pm, on the first Monday of the month you are island hopping in Indonesia. At the precise moment that your mum is waiting for that call, you are at a beach party. In front of you are a lot of very happy people, loads of new friends, maybe a bit of a hunk/babe that you are eyeing up (and the more alcohol you have, the tastier they look!… been there eh!!), a lot of cheap beer, and not a telephone in sight. As for remembering that time on that day in that month… you lost track of time eight days ago when you all decided to hide your watches away, and live by the day, and not by the time. IT HAPPENS!!

So, your mum doesn't get the call, panics a bit, but calms down thinking there must be another explanation. The phone rings. She snaps it up… it's your gran, wondering how you are. Your mum says that you failed to call. She starts to reassure your mum, but brings the subject up of the dangers of travel (false of course). Your mum panics again. All through the week she doesn't sleep as everyone she meets asks her about you, and she says that she is still waiting to hear. They all reassure her, but always seem to add to her worry.

One week later: you get back to the mainland, stay in a hos-

tel, and realise that you are a week late. Ah well, I'm a week late already… so you leave it a couple of days! Finally you ring. You are calmly asked why you didn't ring, but you are so thrilled at what you have just done that thoughts of your parents worry go right over your head. After the call, you go off to the beach/pub, pleased at catching up on news from home, oblivious of the worry. Your mum sits there, relieved, but drained by the worry. What happens next?

And so here we have it… a page in the life of a 'regular phonecaller' who fails to call. I'm as guilty as the next person for not keeping in touch properly, but I hope at least that my parents knew that I would be in touch some time. Your parents will always think the worst, unless you make sure that they know exactly what is going on. Events like this above, which as I'm sure you'll realise are very common, are very unnecessary and avoidable. Just as long as you realise that they will worry, and that it is your 'duty' to keep them informed, you should spare them this. Nuff said!

POST RESTANTE

Post what???? Well this is a system that works extremely well, and one which is very under-utilised for what it is. 'Post Restante' is simply the name of a postal system in which letters that are sent to you stay in the Post Office that they have been sent to, and simply wait for you to pick them up (with the use of identification). If you don't pick it up within their alloted time, which can be anything up to six months, it will be sent 'return to sender'. God knows why it is called Post Restante, daft if you ask me!

How does it work?

Example:

I know that my daughter Claire Sedding will be in Sydney in April:

I therefore address the envelope as follows…

```
AIR MAIL      ■ ■ ■

Miss Claire Sedding
Post Restante,
GPO,
Sydney,
AUSTRALIA.
```

This letter, when it reaches Sydney, will stay there for up to a month, and if not collected it will be sent back 'Return to sender', so remember to put your address on the back of the envelope. In the GPO's they may well publish a list of all the mail which is in, or have a box where it is filed alphabetically for you to sort through. All you need then is your passport, or some form of ID, to pick your post up. The only problem is, for example, with names like mine. Some people call me Thomas Griffiths, others Tom Griffiths (preferred… just to let you know!), some may put T.Griffiths, others T.P.Griffiths, finally, some may put Griffiths Tom/Thomas. These will all be filed under their different alphabetical areas, so it is always worth asking

TOP TIP!

Get them to use brightly coloured envelopes (green/pink,etc.) so your letter is easy to spot and pick out.

people to address with the same title, or end up looking under all possibilities. Definitely not worth friends using your nickname, unless you are expecting it of course.

Basically, wherever you go in the world (just about), if your family or friends write to the main post office (GPO) in whatever town you are staying in, the letter should be held in that post office in the Post Restante area. This obviously depends on how much of the backpacker trail you think that the town is on. Obviously it is better to use capital cities or major towns as collecting points for your mail, as you have more guarantee that you will receive it.

☞ **NB When going to collect your mail make sure that you go to the correct Post Office, as I got caught out on this one. Ask at the Post Office if they have the main/only Post Restante system in the town, and if not find out where you should go.**

Receiving letters

We all like to receive letters, in fact there is nothing better than going to the post office having been away from home for a bit to find a letter or a parcel waiting for you. Simple news from home, or just general chat about things and people that you haven't heard from or seen for a while is one of the best things in the world. So do make sure you sort out a few plans before you shoot off, letting people (as well as your family) know roughly where you'll be and at what time... and get your mates to keep sending those letters!

Keep in touch with travelling friends

This system is also useful for seeing if any of your friends are in town if there is a list published on the wall, or if you have access to the mail. However refrain from writing messages on the letters that may be funny to you and your mate, but appear obscene to their parents for example. Why I say this is that I happened to stumble across a letter for my friend in Ko Samui, Thailand. I left my address on the Island, and a message which I thought was hilarious at the time. Unknown to me... Ben had already left Ko Samui, and had not picked up his mum's letter. Did I hear anyone say Return to Sender? So my hilarious messages... winged their way like a little white dove... back to his mum. Good one Tom! Right comedian you turned out to be!

Post Restante is also very useful for keeping in touch with other backpackers who are also on the move. If you tell friends to expect a letter in Bali for example, even if you arrive a week earlier/later than the other, you will know where they are. If you move on, you can leave a chain of messages at the Post Offices en route, so they can catch you up somewhere. **This system isn't very well publicised, it does work, so do use it.**

TOP TIP!

Arrange to meet a friend in a place overseas. Say you'll leave a message at the Post Restante. When you get there, write the letter to your friend, put a stamp on it, and then leave it in the Post Restante section at the GPO you're in (having got permission to do it first). A great way to leave a message.

American Express Travellers Cheques

I've put this under the Post Restante because if you have AMEX travellers cheques they basically offer the same system. They run a postal service where they will hold post for 3 months for you. You will get a list of their addresses, and they are very reliable.

'Travellers Connections' Voice-mail Services

Think that you're just about ready to bang yourself into the age of technology and use the Post Restante system of the future? Nowadays the world and his dog have got mobile phones, even I've got a pager.

So what is voice-mail?

Dead simple... **it's just like an upmarket answering machine**, except that it is your personal one, and you can operate it from all over the world. As soon as I came across this I knew that it would be a winner. When you subscribe (which if you do it through this book you'll find that you get a great rate with the voucher in the back) you are given your own personal telephone number. **By accessing your number with your security code from anywhere in the world you can leave a recorded message for everyone, and pick up your own messages.**

☞ *For example... 'Hi there, it's now May 8th and I landed in Sydney two days ago. I'm fine and having a fantastic time. I'll be staying at the xxxxxxxxx hostel for a week and then moving on to Byron Bay. If you want to get in touch my number is xxxxxxxxx and I'm in room 21. If you want to write to me, write to the Post Restante in Brisbane, as I'll be there around the beginning of June. Mum you'd love it out here, the beaches are full of hunky Aussie lifeguards... wish you were here? The suntan's coming on well, but then you probably don't want to hear that… well tough! Leave a message as I'd love to hear from you.'*

As you travel around you can change the messages so that everyone can keep track of how you are getting on.

Why is it a fantastic idea?

◆ It is always nice to hear your friend's voices as you travel around… news, gossip, etc.
◆ Family and friends can always check on the progress of your travels.
◆ It can cost you as little as the price of a stamp to keep in touch.
◆ You can use it as a way of meeting up with other travellers… 'I'll be in xxxxx on the 24th… '
◆ No postal delays or worries about time differences.
◆ If you like it you can keep it for use back in the UK for student/work life… as it costs less for the 2nd year.

☛ *For more information see the Ad in the back… get 20% off with this book.*

Foreign relatives/long distance friends

Often have a big temptation to use them as postal/contact points. Beware, sometimes seen by parents as a good idea for you to visit as they don't see much of them. Have you ever met them? Are you just being used as a family 'pawn' to relieve some guilt? Don't get me wrong, it is extremely nice to receive some home comforts when you have been without them for a while. However it can also be extremely awkward, especially if you don't know them too well, as you may feel that you are imposing.

☛ *If you would like to see them, then it is a very good idea to use them as a postal/contact point.*

◆ If not too keen, beware. They may well live 'out in the sticks' somewhere, which may mean splitting up from a group of friends to trek off to them to pick up some post.
◆ You might feel this to be unnecessary and cumbersome at the time, especially if you're forced to play 'catch up' with your mates (although very easy to do).
◆ So, before you go, do check to find if the relative really is 'By a bridge, Up a creek, Timbuctoo', or near to the well beaten backpacker trail.

At this point I can hear a few 'travellers' groaning… of course if they do live

*out in the sticks, it may well be the perfect opportunity for you to see a
real bit of the country. An old family friend of ours (who I'd never met),
lived in the hills behind Surfers Paradise in Australia. Aged 50, she had reap-
peared on the scene on a Harley Davidson motorbike, having had no real
family contact for years. We thought we'd go have a look see! Best decision
we ever made. A real experience, and saw some fantastic Australia that we
would otherwise have missed.*

Postcards

Who hasn't heard the phrase 'Send us a postcard!' It is always said, yet
always laughed off as a joke. But, as you will see from what I have said
before, it is definitely worth doing as it will save parents a lot of anxiety. But
again, on the regularity issue, beware! If your parents are used to them coming at regular intervals, when one doesn't arrive, they may worry. They easily get lost, as they are not seen as priority mail.

This can be avoided by putting them into envelopes – loses the attraction of them, but at least you know that they'll arrive. I laughed at Tony for
having a load of self addressed envelopes in his pack to put postcards in.
However, a few months down the line when a load of mine hadn't arrived,
it suddenly looked like a good idea! Possibly a good idea for you? However,
note that this method is a bit more expensive, as the theory behind the postcard is with it being the cheapest way of keeping in touch.

Your parents may also be more receptive to helping you out when you
return (i.e. with requests for cash) if they know that you made an effort to
remember them. If you do have a dodgy experience, it is probably best not
to tell them before you get home, they'll only worry. I suppose 'What they
don't know won't hurt them', just as long as you don't find yourself in a
position where you need to talk to them about it. Just be careful about
unnecessary worry.

Phone calls

There are phones all over the world now, and in all sorts of isolated places.
Just a quick 10 seconds saying where you are, where you're going, and that
you're fine, and having fun, will make a huge difference. However, if any of
the above are not true, don't ring and try to lie to them, as invariably they
will be able to tell if you are lying. This will make things even worse for
them. **BT Chargecards are an excellent way of keeping in contact like
this.** You can get them so that the only number that it will work for is your
home number, so even if it does get stolen, it won't matter. Lots of 10 second phone calls will not cost too much, and is a small price to pay for peace
of mind. Furthermore they go straight on your parent's bill, so you can pay

as you go and monitor them at the same time. If they are getting too expensive, you can always end the card whenever you want.

Ever thought of taping yourself?

This is something that my family has done for years to keep in touch with Aunty Nicky out in Australia, but I have only just had it mentioned to me recently, and I think that it is definitely worth a mention. We used to use the small Dictaphone tapes, but it is perfectly possible with a normal cassette. After a few months out why not record yourself onto a cassette (you'll easily find somewhere to do it), and then send that to your family. Better than any postcard or letter, and it really will give them a flavour of what you are up to. Well, worth a mention anyway!

And finally...

Thinking that it might well be alright letting your 'little darlings' leave the nest for the wide blue yonder? I hope so! **It's about time that we fell on our arses and learnt to pick ourselves up**. We can do it. We will be all right. After all, you have done it, so why shouldn't we?

Well... what are you waiting for?

CHAPTER 5

Health and Emergencies

'He who has health has hope, and he who has hope has everything.' *Arab Proverb. But what use is 'everything' if you can't experience the joys of being pissed and dancing like a pratt!*

(For general points on Health, *see* '**Tips**' Health.)

This is a serious issue, and needs good discussion before you go

There are obviously general worries about malaria, typhoid, hepatitis, etc., which can be avoided by a few jabs here and there. So make sure you go to your doctor in good time (at least 2 months before you are due to leave).

◆ However, if you are **required to take a drug on a daily basis,** you need a bit of planning. A lot will depend on where you go, and what you are planning to do.

◆ In hot countries, or wet countries you may have **difficulty in keeping your medication dry and protected**.

◆ Can you fit it all in your pack, or will you have to get some sent out to you/pick it up from another country?

◆ **You may not be able to send drugs through the post**, and on many border crossings you may have problems getting them across.

◆ If you are in need of some medication in an emergency, **will it be available where you are going?**

◆ What if it gets lost/damaged?

Problems like these may lead to an undesired abrupt end to your trip, something you obviously won't want.

Planning, and any strategies, are best to be worked out now.

☞ **NB IF YOU HAVE TO CARRY MEDICINE MAKE SURE THAT YOU HAVE A DOCTOR'S NOTE IN CASE YOU ARE STOPPED BY CUSTOMS OR IF YOU NEED TO REPLACE IT.**

Serious problems

If there are any serious problems, **always get in touch with the Embassy straight away on (0171) 273 3000**. If you are required to take any regular medication, something which you may not be able to get in a foreign country, then you may need to have it sent out to you. If this is the case then you may require a special licence to have it sent through the post. For further information on this ring (0171) 273 3806. If you do this in good time, then you will hopefully be able to sort out the paperwork now, rather than having to wait somewhere while all the paperwork goes through. Having tried a dummy run of this myself as a bit of research for this book, I was passed all over the place, and found that there is probably a lot of bureaucracy to get through.

However I have been assured that in the event of an emergency the

Embassy will be very efficient and treat each case separately... so don't think that you should worry too much.

GOVERNMENTAL HELP AND THE EMBASSY SYSTEM

What the British Consul CAN do...

- ◆ issue emergency passports
- ◆ contact relatives or friends to ask them to help you with money/tickets
- ◆ advise on how to transfer funds
- ◆ in emergency can advance money against a sterling cheque for up to £100 supported by a banker's card valid for the appropriate amount
- ◆ as a last resort make a repayable loan for repatriation to the UK (exceptional circumstances)
- ◆ help you get in touch with local lawyers, interpreters and doctors
- ◆ arrange for next of kin to be informed in event of accidents or a death and advise on procedures
- ◆ contact and visit British nationals under arrest or in prison
- ◆ make representations on your behalf to the local authorities in certain circumstances

But a Consul CANNOT...

- ◆ intervene in court proceedings
- ◆ get you out of prison
- ◆ give legal advice or instigate court proceedings on your behalf
- ◆ get you better treatment in hospital/prison than is provided for local nationals
- ◆ investigate a crime
- ◆ pay your hotel, legal, medical, or any other bills
- ◆ pay for travel tickets for you except in very special circumstances
- ◆ undertake work more properly done by travel representatives, airlines, banks or motoring organisations
- ◆ obtain accommodation, work or a work permit for you
- ◆ formally assist dual nationals in the country of their second nationality

HELLO MR EMBASSY MAN.
COULD YOU PLEASE PHONE
MY DAD AND ASK HIM TO
SEND MY LUCKY SLIPPERS!!

EMBASSY

Consular Advice

This is simply what you would naturally do if you have any problems abroad... get yourself to the nearest Embassy. It is very unlikely that you will need their assistance, however if you do, **ask for it**, as that is what they are there for... **to look after your interests while you are abroad.**

Good preparation Before you Go
Get full medical insurance
Be aware of the laws and obey them
When you land in a country find the address of your nearest Consul... can be found at the airport Information places, at the hostels, in the phone books, etc.
Have fun and enjoy yourself

People with Diabetes

The thought of travel may be appealing to you, but nerves and worries may well put you off. However travelling with diabetes *is* possible, and to give you a few thoughts, ideas and guidelines, Ben (my diabetic travelling specialist!) has a few points to make... 'Providing you've done your homework the diabetic traveller has nothing to worry about'

◆ do make sure that any travelling companions understand generally about diabetes and the difference between being 'Hypo' and 'Hyper', as you well know the dangers but they won't. They need to know what to do in an emergency, especially if you are pissed!

Be aware of your 3 main concerns:

1. Supply
◆ how to get fresh supplies of insulin halfway up a mountain in the Andes.
◆ how do I keep my insulin cool.
◆ what supplies do I need for my blood-glucose testing kit.
◆ how will my equipment stand up to the job in hand.
◆ can electronics/insulin withstand extreme heat/cold, bright sunlight, water immersing shock, x-ray, etc. Answer is often no (check with the care team).

2. Safety and security
◆ for obvious reasons you don't want others to either steal or use your needles.

3. General health
◆ What if things go horribly wrong?

♦   What if I contract dysentery and can't eat?
♦   What if I have to go to hospital?
♦   What if I can't find enough carbohydrate and have a hypo in a remote area?

How well you respond to these problems depends on your personality and the amount of time you have to prepare for the literally hundreds of scenarios you might have to face on your travels. If you treat it proactively as part of the adventure, you'll be fine. Get scared or panic, and you'll end up in trouble.

☞   *Know yourself and your equipment and think creatively around the problem.*

♦   **Before travelling consult your GP about using an insulin pen if you don't already.** These are simple, clean, effective, and safe in that it is easy to spot if it has been tampered with... and rugged... imagine dicking around with glass phials of insulin in the middle of the Kalahari! Also easier to get through customs unnoticed. Furthermore you only need to worry about the needle heads that go with them (packs of 100 at the time of writing cost about £8), so make sure you take a needle clipper with you. Whichever bits you take as optional extras, these bits are the most important.
♦   **It is vital to keep insulin cool.** The best way is to take some tough container and store the insulin + needles at the bottom of your backpack (coolest place)
♦   Keep it with you at all times, don't be tempted to put it in the hostel/hotel fridge
♦   Store it overnight in some ice or cold water
♦   Kiddies thermos flasks (non glass) are very useful, one for wet (insulin pens in cold water), one for dry (needles, etc.)
♦   Another idea may be to sew storage pockets into the inside of your backpack, making sure that they are well padded
♦   Freezer packs are another idea, may be worth taking.
♦   Only carry the insulin stick that you are using at the time, and perhaps one spare, likewise with needle heads (assuming use of the pens) in the open at any one time
♦   If you feel your insulin security to have been breached at any time... play it safe, clip the needle, and chuck it away... it's not worth the risk of any kind of infection.
♦   **Tip:** if you carry a shoulder slung pouch with you with all your 'goodies' in, at a push you can put it under your clothes at any moment of 'dodginess'.

☞   *Always remember that this stuff keeps you alive!*

ᴜpply

As it's only possible to carry 2/3 months supply of insulin at a time, why not get a load of your favourite goodies and see whether or not the Foreign Office can help with its transportation to one of the Embassies on your route. If you can arrange for something to be sorted out before you go, whereby you know that as soon as you get down to your last supplies you'll be able to pick up some more on your way, then you'll have your own peace of mind and peace of mind for your family. I have looked into this, and I've found that each case will be treated specially… so I believe that if you put your case over strongly enough, the Embassies will help you out the best that they can. The numbers to use are on page 47 and at the back of the book.

In dire need of any sort, head straight for the nearest British Embassy

ᴮlood testing kits

The best types have a little door which can keep the rain off, and are rugged enough for taking with you. The versions by Boehringer and Mannheim (providing they don't get too wet) are OK. Take an immersion bag to keep these in, and Lowe Alpine does a nice washbag which is convenient for the bits and pieces associated. This can pack into around 250-300g.

General health

It is imperative for any travellers with diabetes to have a health check up before you go. Newly diagnosed people with diabetes should probably wait until things have settled down before going anywhere too adventurous… but again it is a question of how well you adapt both mentally and physically.

Enjoying yourself

- Avoid quick carbohydrates at the wrong times.
- Alcohol, although a carbohydrate, reduces blood sugar and so increases the chance of a Hypo. The key therefore is to get a good, starchy meal of bread, rice, or pasta down your neck before getting hammered.
- Narcotics such as amphetamines and ecstasy are definitely out if you're stupid enough to take them, as they affect the metabolic rate.
- Make sure you have sweets or chocolate handy at all times and you'll be fine.

The above information has been checked and approved by the British Diabetic Association.

51

Advice from the BDA

Before travelling contact your diabetes care team and GP.
Have a health check.
Plan your Insulin and Test Strip supplies.

Things to consider:
◆   Identification
◆   Insurance – one that doesn't rule out pre-existing conditions
◆   Illness – make sure you and your companions know what to do
◆   What to take – how to store insulin in transit
◆   Travelling through time zones
◆   The effects of extremes of temperature/altitude/bright sunlight on insulin and equipment.
◆   Physical activity – adjusting insulin/food intake to more/less activity.
◆   Foot care – examine reguarly, seek early treatment for all foot problems.
◆   Food – not always available when needed, carry plenty of carbohydrates.
◆   Fluids – Diet drinks not always available. Alcohol effects your blood sugar – never drink on an empty stomach.

If you have any questions, they are very happy for you to get in touch with them on (0171) 636 6112 (The BDA Careline) or write to the:
British Diabetic Association,
10, Queen Anne Street,
London W1M OBD
Tel: (0171) 323 1531 Fax: (0171) 637 3644

TOP TIP!

Do get in touch anyway as they produce a number of travel guides, advice booklets and vital information for many different countries.

I'm not qualified to give answers, so take time to look into health issues properly

I really don't have many answers to any difficulties that you may have in this area. It is such a massive field that I wouldn't be able to do it justice, so I won't even attempt it. However there are a couple of numbers/addresses at the back of the book that you may like to try. Good luck to you! In most developed countries you will find no real problems, as many, like Australia, have a 'tit for tat' system with the UK. You will be covered under their health system, and so will receive good care. However *medical insurance* (*see* **Tips**) is *essential* and will need looking into fully to find the right policy for any special requirements, so you don't find yourself uninsured due to any small print.

Accidents may, and will, happen – they do in your everyday life – but we all come back safely, maybe just a little 'misshapen' than before. I can bear testament to that, having got 5 stitches in my head, after accidentally putting it in a ceiling fan (long story – but I was stone cold sober at the time. If ever you go to the Twenty Degrees South Hostel in Airlie Beach, Australia, do look for a dented fan on one of the ceilings in one of the rooms, autographed by yours truly!). The stitches were very expensive at the time, but I got the money back from the Australian government, which I thought was fantastic... more beers for me!

Illness on return

Beware of contagious bacterial infection. A girlfriend of mine once came back from Pakistan with a magnificent dose of Giardia (Amoebic Dysentery), and whilst her mother played the fantastic part of Florence Nightingale, she unfortunately came down with it as well... not a pleasant experience at all, as they were both very ill. From time to time, these contagious diseases may be picked up, so it is always best to be vigilant and in touch with a doctor, as the symptoms are often disguised as other things.

Good preparation before you go will leave you ready for anything, and help you deal with any situation that arises. And when you get back, make sure that the only thing you've brought back with you is a suntan!

CHAPTER 6

Male solo

'Step into a new world... step out a new man.'
Billy Connolly.

So you're probably thinking... is this really a good idea?

Will I be isolated? Will I be lonely? Many will tend to say that it really depends on the sort of person that you are in fact, I tend to agree. As a confident person who has absolutely no qualms about going up to anyone and starting a conversation, travelling solo was an easy option for me. **However do remember that on my first trip I was accompanied by a friend of**

mine. Originally I was up for going it alone, however going with a long time school mate seemed to be a better idea for me at the time, although he nearly dropped out at the last minute... but that's Tony and women for you! However I have met many people who have left their home country with a shyness that you wouldn't believe, a courageous step for which they always have my full admiration, and have been totally transformed into confident, easy going people. Mind you, for someone to take a big step like this means that they must have a strong willingness to succeed anyway, which always seems to help!

You're all in the same boat!

It is easy to forget that whilst travelling everyone is in the same boat, and it is in fact extremely easy to introduce yourself to strangers and make friends. In hostels and bars all over the world there is a kind of common language learnt and spoken by all... ' Hi I'm xxxx from xxxxxxxx, mind if I join you? So what's your name, and where are you from?' There are no catchy one liners that we all learnt as kids and sweat over in clubs and pubs... that is if you have the courage to even make the first move. In fact for many it may even be a little odd introducing yourself to someone of the same sex! Suddenly meeting people takes on a whole new perspective and meaning, in fact a skill that I believe will be a great asset to you in life.

Working as a barman many people have commented about how well I can hold a decent conversation with a stranger at such a young age, a useful skill to have. But this is not just to do with my own confidence, but more to do with meeting people whilst travelling, even more so when I was on my own hitching across Canada. When you get into other people's cars they want to know your whole life story before you get out (I can hear my friends saying '... and I bet you gave it to them Tom... !'). You are forced into a position where you have to learn to converse with people well. From then on, it all comes naturally.

The message is therefore simple... **yes it is very easy to meet people and make friends, and you will make friends everywhere you go**. In fact if you're the kind of chatterbox like myself (as all of my friends will testify to... but I've got a great personality!) then you'll perhaps make too many friends and have trouble keeping up with them all.

The advantage of being solo.

The advantage of being on your own therefore lies in the fact that **you can come and go as you please**... meet up with whoever you want (and whoever you don't want), and go wherever you want to go without having to consult and discuss it with a partner first. If you meet a nice group of

Swedish ladies, who want to whisk you off sailing round some tropical islands for a few days… you go! You'll find that you'll join up with groups of people, travel for a bit, and then meet up with others to travel with later on. Depending on the pace of the travelling of the different groups, you'll always be meeting up with someone or other 'down the road' somewhere. In most countries travelling is very easy, too easy in fact in places such as the east coast of Australia, South East Asia, etc. Very good friends will be made and kept… you'll be able to meet up in other countries if your paths cross again by use of the Post Restante system mentioned in chapter 4. And when everything is over you'll have reunion parties to look forward to all over the world with your new 'international' address book.

☛ *Therefore in answering the questions 'will I be isolated and lonely?'… only if you try really hard to be by yourself, if not… you've got to be joking haven't you?*

Of course if you make no effort to introduce yourself to people and become a quiet recluse wherever you go, things may be different. But 99% of the time you will find this impossible, as everyone is in the same boat, and so you all get to know each other.

Travelling from place to place.

Again this is made easy by the people you will meet. Yes, the guide books are extremely useful, and worth getting for information on places to go and stay, however you'll find your route determined mainly by other people. They'll have been to places you're about to go to, and vice-versa, in that you've been to where they want to go. Over a few beers you'll swap stories, information, etc. about where it is best to be at that time, what there is to see and do, the best bars/clubs, beaches, etc, etc. You'll probably find your plans changing from day to day... which to me is the beauty and attraction of travelling.

Every day is different, and you really don't know what is going to happen tomorrow. We have all made the common mistake of initially saying that we will be here for a week, there for two, this country for a month, and returning home on this or that day. Yes it is vital to make those general plans before you go when sorting your ticket out, **but be prepared for those plans to change... but most importantly let them change**. As you have all the time in the world, you'll find that you'll regret not postponing your departure from Bali so you could stay on for a couple of weeks to visit the Indonesian Islands with your friends. Go with the flow... but do remember to divide your time properly as you don't want to be left with only a week on your ticket, £5 to your name, and the whole of South East Asia to cover!

As I mentioned in my introduction... (if you've read it that is!), my friend Tim is testament to travel changes. Having graduated from Sheffield University with a good degree he worked in England over the summer and then left on a Round the World trip, intending, as he thought, to be back in June. It is now next March, he is having an absolute ball out there in Australia, and as far as I can see, has no real reason to come back for a while. Jealous? Of course I am! 6 months can easily change to 9 or 12. You are only really constrained if you have to come back for college... some don't, but I really wouldn't advise this.

☛ *If you've worked hard enough to get into college, why throw it all away??*

Time to slow your life down

If you've just graduated and the 'world is your oyster', as long as the finances hold, many do end up travelling for 3, 4, 5, or even 6 years! It is inevitable that you will get the 'Travel Bug'... and not the one that keeps you on the toilet for 2 weeks (although a quick dose of that might come your way if you're lucky... remember that Lomotil/Diafed in your First Aid Kit!). When the bug hits you'll just want to travel on and on! Your home country will seem so far away and unimportant that you'll find you'll enter this kind of relaxed state of mind as you leave the 'rat race' far behind.

'The Fijian Experience'

The experience I'm talking about first happened to me in Fiji. For the past four years I had worked very hard for every exam that I took, right the way through GCSE's and A levels. The time spent after my A Levels was in working at McDonalds, every shift and hour possible. The whole lot was just hectic hectic hectic, all at a very fast pace of life! First stop was Los Angeles, a city, and a very fast moving city at that. After that it was Hawaii, again 'stress city' with the amount of Americanism and Japanese tourism there. To tell you the truth we couldn't wait to get out of these two places quick enough. So still in a kind of 'hurry, rush, speed' kind of a mood, we landed in Fiji... *stop!*

In Fiji they have this remarkable thing called '*Fiji time*', and it is absolutely fantastic! If the bus driver bothers to get up in the morning... then there will be a bus! If not, then you might have to wait a couple of hours for him to turn up. The true Fijians are incredibly friendly, but sincere with it, and just laugh at all the tourists trying to rush around the islands. I guess you find exactly the same in areas like the Caribbean, and to some extent right on our doorstep in the Republic of Ireland. This relaxed atmosphere *forces* you to relax... and you do! **I think Tony and I fully realised at that point that it was possibly the first time that we had ever properly relaxed**, I mean *really slowed down*. You always hear people saying about how relaxed they think they are. But if you ask them what they'll be doing at 11 o'clock on Wednesday morning, or 6.30pm on Friday night, you'll usually get an answer.

☛ *Your life is 'ordered' and your own little world is revolving around you without you realising it.*

Is this what they call culture shock?

The state of mind that I'm talking about which we experienced when in Fiji, and so for the rest of our trip, is one in which you really don't know what is going to happen that afternoon, let alone next Friday night. It's a weird, but extremely nice feeling... it's almost as if you're experiencing the so called 'rat race' in every country you visit, **but as a spectator**, sitting at the side and watching everything go by. You'll start to notice the difference between the countries, and between the different people who live side by side within these countries. But more importantly you'll start to notice differences between your country and theirs, and maybe even start to appreciate your own country more, and the differences that exist throughout the world. I guess this is what they call culture, and the realisation that you are undergoing one of those infamous 'culture shocks'! I'm not one of those 'yeah right on man' travellers, I just appreciate what is around me, and the difference between people and their environments.

You'll always hear people talking knowledgeably about the poverty out in Africa and Asia for example. **But as far as I'm concerned you won't really appreciate it until you witness it**. For example we were in a water taxi in Bangkok, a fast little speed boat that flies around the rivers of the city... we were worried about being splashed by the tiny drops of stinking milky white water that lie stagnating in the river. However as we moved on we noticed that the people who live in the shanty towns at the side of the river use it to wash in, for toiletry purposes, and even to wash their food in! Yes I know it is a way of life that they are used to, *but to think that we didn't even want to be splashed by this water*... a reflection of our culture and just how lucky we really are.

Having relatively nothing with you, and living off as cheap a budget as you can... yet still living like a King/Queen in some of the poorer countries, really makes you appreciate where you come from, and your well-off position in this world. It also trivialises a lot of things, and makes you realise that to be happy you don't need piles of money, you just need to do what you enjoy in life, and to appreciate the world around you.

So what am I trying to get at here?

This is where I feel my 'real' education is from, learning to understand people and what they believe in... which is made even easier by travelling solo, as you have no other influences on your thoughts. I also believe it makes you more aware of yourself, who you are, and what role you play in society. As for myself, I've really learnt how lucky I am in relation to others in this world. This is something you can't change. But the important thing is that you are aware of the fact, which I believe makes you a broader and better person, as you escape the narrowness of just thinking about yourself and your own little world. That is my belief, others may, and do, think different-ly. All I am trying to say is that by the time you return you will be a differ-ent/better person... which is a nice thought, eh?

My personal experience of travelling solo.

Yes it can be lonely on the very odd occasion, and although you are going to meet loads of other travellers you may well get stuck with a few that you don't find the easiest to get on with. However in our experience, because you do have this freedom to do exactly what you want, you can easily avoid these ones, and hook up with friends that you do instantly click with, and have a laugh. An added advantage of travelling solo is that you do get to meet more local people, and you'll often get invited into, and become part of a community somewhere. You'll be the 'new boy' in town, be a bit of a star, a known person, and receive all the hospitality that you can cope with. It's an experience that you'll never forget... warmth and friendliness from total strangers. You'll be 'mothered' and looked after, treated to this, and treated to that.

My expression is 'What goes around comes around'. When in Canada, as I had very little money, I lived off the kindness of people. I have never begged, hinted, or made people feel guilty. My plan was to go as far as I could on the money that I had, and simply return home when the pot ran dry. However I didn't need to as I met kindness practically everywhere I went.

☛ *By being agreeable, polite and, as far as I saw it, a good representative of my country... I was literally offered the earth.*

I had strangers sharing camping slots with me, buying me dinner/beers, putting me up overnight... even when there was somewhere else for me to go! It was all insisted on me, and it made me feel great. I guess you think that I'm working for the Canadian Tourist Board! Maybe I should write to them, show them this last bit, and demand some kind of royalty! I've tried to keep in touch with all of these people, and now have many new Canadian friends.

You can't buy kindness, but you can show and exchange it... 'What goes around comes around!'. I'll do the same for them if they come over here in the future, and have already done the same for others over here... picking up hitch-hikers and going out of my way for them, as others have done for me (one guy in Canada picked me up on his way home from work, and insisted on driving me an hour past his turning, simply because I was doing what he had always wanted to do, but had never done!)

Lonely?

No way... on this 13 week trip I probably made up to 10 new friends *each day*, it was impossible not to meet people and make friends, as others want to get to know you, and like to help you. I know Canada is a very civilised place, but wherever you go in the world, you can either be by yourself, or with others.

☛ *This is your choice and your freedom... something you don't really have when travelling with a companion.*

CHAPTER 7

Female solo

"The woman who goes alone can start today; but she who travels with another must wait till that other is ready."
Adapted from Henry David Thoreau (1854) by Tom Griffiths (1997) to suit text.

For the first time in my life I'm going to have to say that this American has actually made a bit of sense. Furthermore, he still makes sense over a century later! The advantage of travelling solo? Well, he's hit the nail right on the head. Independence. Go when you want, where you want, with no-one or nothing holding you back.

☛ **So what's stopping you? Go! Off Round the World, by yourself. Piece of cake. Loads of other women have done it by themselves, so why shouldn't you? You'll be all right!**

Is this what you are thinking at the moment?

If so, good for you. However as you well know, and I'm sure it's at the back of your mind at the moment... it's easy enough to say that whilst sitting in the warmth, comfort and safety of your room, whilst dreaming of hot, golden, sandy beaches in places that you probably haven't even heard of, let alone spell!

◆ Have you got what it takes?
◆ Are you confident enough?
◆ Will you enjoy it, or would you prefer to have the company of a friend for companionship and added security?
◆ What are you looking for in this trip?.

If these are some of the questions that you've been asking yourself for a while, or just starting to ask yourself, then I hope this chapter will be of some use to you. I want all young people who go off travelling to have an absolute ball, and an amazing and unforgettable experience. However this will only happen if you get it right from the start. It is not up to me to say to you... OK you should travel with a friend, and you over there, yes you with the striped flares and the dyed hair, you should travel by yourself.

☞ *Similarly it is for you to make and take that decision, and no-one else.*

The world of advice!

As a young lady about to go off travelling the world by yourself, you are about to discover the world of fantastic advice. Everyone you will possibly know will give you the benefit of their advice/experience whether you want it or not! You may be undergoing this at the moment... isn't it just the biggest pain in the arse! Your dad wants you to go off and broaden your mind, but to be careful while you are doing it. Your mum just thinks that you are going to be raped, killed or both. Your granny keeps on going on about how in her day young women would find a nice young man, settle down and hold the house together and not go gallivanting off around the world like a young hussy. But she's still given you a £5 note to go off and buy a rucksack, unaware how prices have risen since the war!

As for everyone else, well, they were watching the news during Christmas 1996, and like everybody were horrified at the young backpacker who was killed by the monk in Thailand. Suddenly they are the foremost knowledge on the subject of young women travelling by themselves, or at all for that matter. Why don't you ask them the circumstances of the death... "Probably to do with the fact that she was a woman travelling alone and so was naturally asking for it!" Point proved, eh? Unfortunately the young lady decided to resist whilst being mugged. So what happens in the same circumstances in places like London, Manchester, Liverpool and Glasgow? Do our muggers turn round and say "I'm terribly sorry to bother you but could you give me some money... no?... pleeease?... oh, go on... pleeeease?... well, I can only try... goodbye, mind how you go!"

NO.

Let's put things in perspective for a moment

The point I'm trying to make is that unfortunately in life bad things happen. I've been mugged, and I'm sure a few of you out there are in the same boat. Yes it was nasty, I didn't enjoy it one bit. I was 16, and on my own in France. Shit happens! The only difference, apart from the obvious, was that she was female, and travelling by herself. The press need a story, it's on the news, suddenly every female backpacker in the world is at risk.

Have you ever heard Trevor McDonald saying... "and finally on the news tonight, 20,000 female backpackers were said to be all well and having a fantastic time all over the world tonight, which we are all very happy about. That's all from...".

As I mention later on in the book, you are more likely to be mugged or have things happen to you in your own environment back in your home town, than you are abroad. The simple reason is that you are more aware of your surroundings when you are in unfamiliar territory, whereas at home you tend to become unaware of everything that is around you... because it always *is*!

You'll be fine!

I think you're aware of what I'm getting at now. You will be fine. You will be safe. I mean, you're very unlikely to put yourself in a dangerous/compromising situation are you! There are thousands of females who travel alone, just like there are thousands of blokes who travel alone. The general tip is **don't worry**, you'll meet people as soon as you get on the plane. Jane for example pretends to hate flying, and then gets the guy next to her to hold her hand on take off. Always one for a good icebreaker is our Jane! By the time you land you'll probably have met others on the plane, if not you'll meet them at the first hostel anyway. **From then on in, you'll find that you'll never be alone unless you really want to be**.

Coming back to the independence bit, this is where you'll find your advantage lies. If you want to be by yourself, you can. If you want to be a social butterfly, it is all too easy to bounce from one set of friends to another. Go sailing with this group, scuba diving with that one, and then skinny dipping with 5 hunky Australian lifeguards when the mood takes you! Everywhere you go you'll meet up with loads of people. Everyone is in the same boat.

The name of the game?... meeting people and having a laugh!

Wherever you go you'll find that there are hundreds of trips organised for you. At every stop, and at every hostel you'll find offers for everything from whale watching, koala spotting, scuba diving, turtles hatching... to bungy, rafting, skydiving, horseriding... I could go on all day if you wanted me to... reef surfing, camping trips, beer factory tours, island tours, watersports, etc., etc., etc. Do it all! I'm getting excited just thinking about it, so I'm sure that you are too. But the main thing about it is that you'll meet loads of other backpackers on these trips too.

☞ *You are all doing the same thing, so just sit back and enjoy it!*

Let's cut the faffing around and get on to the useful stuff!

I hope now that you've got the confidence and conviction that it is possible for you to travel alone. It is a lot easier than most of you realise. Once you've decided that you've got this confidence to get up and get on with sorting out your travel arrangements, you'll realise that **good planning** will mean the difference between living your dreams, or confronting your nightmares. However you are not indestructible, infallible, or immortal (even though it would be great if you were... you'd have all sorts of men after you!) so don't expect it all to be too much of a piece of cake, as you do still have to look after yourself.

Packing

For a good backpack, pack, divide in two, re-pack, and divide in two again. Then do a preliminary re-pack. Once packed, ask where the scales are hidden in the house, and then weigh your pack. *At this point you may well come across a dilemma with the realisation of the fact that the scales don't actually lie, and that you will be forced to agree with them!* Having weighed the pack don't be tempted to weigh yourself. As long as you're happy, what does it matter what anyone else thinks anyway? And if any man says any different, give him hell... he'll soon learn to keep his mouth shut and opinions to himself anyway!

Finally you should try and get your pack down to **no more than about 8kg**. You really should be ruthless at this stage and ask yourself whether you really do need three pairs of 'going out' shoes. If you've really got to ask yourself these questions, you probably don't need them, so throw them out.

Trust me (how many times have you heard that from a man, eh?) when we (myself and the girls) say that you are going to collect a lot of things on the way. Your pack will get bigger, and it will get heavier. So unless you have the muscles of an Albanian goat-herders wife, **do yourself a favour now and pack as light as possible**. The girls have devised an additional 'think about' list below to go with the one under **"Packing"**, so have a look and a little think about it. If it does come to over 8kg don't worry too much, you'll be able to send things home en route if it gets too heavy. But don't be put off collecting those little momentos, as a few years down the track they are the little reminders that will bring it all flooding back to you! Happy days!

Do you have a backpack?

If the answer is no and you don't know much about them, and the thought of lugging one around sounds as appetising as a snog with Andrew Lloyd Webber... don't panic! There are actually backpacks designed for women which you might prefer. Do remember that you have to carry it around with you all the time, so make sure you shop around for something that you find comfortable, and which isn't going to fall apart on you a couple of weeks in to the trip. **If anything is worth spending money on before you go, this is it.** Remember the Millets discount and have a look at the Vango 'Exodus' 55 with its adjustable back (fits your shape exactly), and the Eurohike 'Adventure 55' (cheaper) which packs flat and converts into a suitcase with its 'zip away' straps, this will give you an idea of what is on the market. Don't be fobbed off with your dad's old Scout, heavy duty, green, canvas rucksack. Sure, you can throw it under a car doing 100 mph and it'll survive, but as soon as it gets heavy it'll hurt your back and you'll regret taking it.

What pearly Tips have we got for you?

Confidence

Every girl that I have met travelling has exuded confidence. Whether they have it or not, they showed it. If you are a naturally confident person, this will be natural for you anyway. You'll ask for things, go up to people and introduce yourself, join in, find your way around, and damn well get whatever, or to wherever, you want. If you are not a naturally confident person you will be doing exactly the same, except that you'll be doing all this a bit slower than the 'naturals'. But don't worry, because the change in you will happen. **You don't need to force it, it just happens.**

The environment is totally different, everyone's attitudes are different, and you'll soon learn by what everyone else does. It is a very harmless transformation that you'll find will come very naturally to you. **Your confidence is there inside, it just takes a relaxed and unpressured lifestyle for it all to come out.** Additionally, a change from your usual surroundings/mates tends to help. From the age of maybe 11 upwards you will be in groups of friends. Maybe you are one of the 'leaders' of the group, or a 'follower' in the group. Whichever it was should be of no difference... that was all 'kids stuff'! When you travel, age, race, and height on the social ladder make absolutely no difference.

You will very rarely wear make up. Sometimes you may go for a week without looking in a mirror. Vanities go, weight becomes irrelevant, and looks become so much less important. **Suddenly people take you for who you are, not what you look like,** or for who you pretend/would like to be. This seems to be the big lesson that people learn. The result is more confidence in the person that is really inside you, and so a stronger character. In terms of travelling you'll walk confidently in the street, be assertive, make decisions, be spontaneous, etc, etc.

TOP TIP!

Always look as though you know where are going, even when hopelessly lost. You are therefore less of a target as you look less vulnerable. You will exude confidence, to the point that it will smack people in the face from 20 yards!

Wedding ring

Essential item. The most important item. Get one! It doesn't have to be an expensive one, in fact make sure that it isn't worth anything. All you need is an accessory which can be used in pretence if needed. As long as you don't have any superstitions, then simply slipping it on in times of need does the job perfectly. A wedding ring, a few blatant lies, and a bit of acting, will get you absolutely everywhere and always out of trouble. Your husband will be meeting you at the 'next stop'. Your husband is just 'over there', as you con-

fidently walk over to some nice young man/men who you may/may not have met, sit down, and with ease, move out of a sticky situation. The fact that you are seen as another man's property might help to keep unwanted attention at bay. Very useful, but imperative that it accompanies you at all times.

Leave a record of your stay

And I don't mean by pulling every available man in the building, or by smashing all the crockery in a drunken impression of your favourite Greek night in Swanage! In all the hotels, hostels, and backpacker places there is always somewhere where you can leave some sort of record of the date of your visit, and even an indication of where you are off to next, and with whom. Try not to make strict plans to meet up with friends or relatives en route from home before you go, as you will find invariably that your plans will change. You may then find it difficult/impossible to be there through no fault of your own. If you're late and various people/relatives are expecting news back home you really will cause a lot of unnecessary anxiety and worry.

I hope this backs up what I have said in the section 'Keeping in Touch' under **"Parents"**. These are good reasons for not sending postcards at a regular interval, and for not promising to send letters and postcards on certain

Leave a record of your stay

dates. If you forget, or leave your parents waiting for news, then they'll only think the worst. Whereas you'll be off exploring tropical islands with no Post Office for hundreds of miles... but do they know that? **"I'll be in touch" normally does the trick... especially if you are!** As for meeting up with people en route, and keeping in touch, remember 'Post Restante' (outlined under 'Parents') and the American Express postal service.

Asking for help

Obvious? Then why do people always wander around saying "We'll find it in a minute, I know it's around here somewhere!" Is it just a British thing where we're too polite to stop people and ask for their help? The Americans are very good at doing this... maybe this is the price we have to pay for a culture! Asking for help saves so much wasted time. If I turn up in a town, starving, but lost... I usually go to a bar/restaurant and ask the barmen and waiters where they go for something to eat/drink. You'll automatically find yourself in an area where all the young people tend to 'hang out', again meaning that you're not in the wrong place, and so you don't stick out as a tourist. Often in these situations you will find yourself invited to parties, etc. as you are recognised as a newcomer to the area.

Ask for everything... you'll never miss out, and if you don't ask, you don't get. It'll also save you a lot of time. I know you'll have all the time in the world, but that's not the point!

Be aware of potential hassles

If you are aware of them, and somehow expect them, then the theory is that they shouldn't be too bad if they happen. On the odd occasion in Third World countries you will be exposed to the crush of touts, hustlers, salesmen and children offering you everything from a room, to food, watches, bracelets, drugs and sex... well anything really! Once you've had a bit of travel experience under your belt, you'll find the situation fairly easy to deal with.

However, if you land in Delhi, Bangkok, Marrakech, etc. fresh from 'Jolly Old England', totally unprepared, **boy are you in for a shock!** At this point you may well be grateful for reading Tips – Chill out, and Locals. If not you may well have the desire to beat a retreat faster than the Allies at Dunkirk, and jump on the first plane home... it happens!

TOP TIP!

This is a waste, and can easily be avoided by doing these countries last, after warming up in countries such as Australia, USA, and Europe first. Go anti-clockwise round the world if in doubt.

The other way of course is to 'bite the bullet' and go for it. It can be very daunting for the first time, but is more harmless than it seems. It is the fact that you are surrounded by a lot of people who think that because you are from a developed country that you have a lot of money. When you think about it, you may well find that you do have a lot of money in relation to the great majority of them.

Try and put it in perspective – usually helps me

The tugging at you from all directions is just a way of them getting your attention, as they don't speak your language. All the 'babbling' in a foreign language, which is as far from the Grade B in GCSE French you got as you can be, is only their 'business talk', discussing the deals they could give you. However your paranoia in these situations forces you to believe that they are plotting your demise! They're not savages you know, they're hardly likely to talk about assassinating you in front of everyone! **Nevertheless you must try and avoid being ripped off, and watch for pick-pockets who take advantage of these swarming crowds.**

You will not be harmed in situations like these, they are just after your business. However do take care to check the situation out properly before getting in taxis, and check out the room before you pay for it. If you don' like it, go elsewhere. Don't be afraid to pay more for your own peace o' mind.

Blondes beware!

Not only because Mr. Mortimer is now single again and loves to 'shark' you, but because a lot of men in some countries tend to be fascinated by your hair. In countries where there are very few/no blondes, a lot of men will have no qualms about coming up to you and touching your head. Jane, for example, also found that many felt that they had the right to get you in to bed, and would not take no for an answer... you know what I mean, ten to two at your local night-club as the slow songs come on!

I shouldn't really joke around the subject, as **a lot of blondes feel very intimidated and threatened in areas such as Africa, India, South East Asia and the Middle East**. You're bound to. In India Jane was unlucky enough to travel with another blonde. It did turn out to be a bad experience... a lot of staring, touching, and this fascination for sex. She believes it is a lot to do with the huge amounts of Western porn that they get over there, leading to many believing that they can simply walk up to a white women and she will simply jump into bed with them.

This is detrimental to Indian men, but unfortunately true. Being from a developed country you have a freedom that their women don't, and therefore they'll be interested in you. Respect their understanding and culture as you are in their country. "It is not especially frightening, just bloody annoying! Ignore them is the best advice, as trying to stop them doing it is just seen as a 'come on'." You'll probably find yourself travelling with a group of people anyway. But if in doubt, don't be proud, just hook up with some people for a while. No worries!

Victorian maid shows ankle to chimney sweep scandal!

Remember that this still happens in a lot of countries, especially the Muslim ones, so wrap up! Your G-String and skimpy bra top may look fantastic on the beaches of the South of France (and in my imagination), but may not go down too well upon entering some of Asia's most sacred buildings... the Taj Mahal being a classic example! Also avoid topless sunbathing, shorts, sleeveless tops, hot pants, etc. in certain countries. Do get advice before you go, and cover up to avoid any hassles. You are a guest in their country, so it is always polite to abide by the rules. In hot countries cover up with loose fitting cotton garments to keep cool... or sweat like a pig (do whatever you feel most comfortable doing!). I know that all this will seem extremely Victorian to you, and perhaps unfair, but then you must realise that you are only visiting, their women have to live with it. But then I suppose that if you know no different?

Breasts

Can shock, even in this country. Similarly, for me to use it as a title like I have above will cause a few raised eye-brows. Just as you wouldn't walk around with them on display in Woolworths (or any other high street store for that matter), shoulders and legs exposed can cause equal discomfort, anger and embarrassment in many countries. Conservatism is the word of the day, especially when you come up against any officials, and definitely when applying for visa extensions, at borders, etc. Sorry girls!

OK enough said, let's conclude this little bit Tom

Cathy is blonde, and spent some time out in some Middle Eastern countries. Having spoken to her, she spoke some sweet pearly words of wisdom! She seemed to encounter most of the things a young female traveller might come up against and so I have asked 'My little Cathy' for some 'top tips' and so here they are:

Cathy's TOP TIPS!

DO:
- *Wear a sober coloured headscarf.*
- *Try and blend in as much as possible.*
- *Be aware of what's going on around you.*
- *Be cynical of helpful strangers, especially male ones.*
- *Ask women for directions/help.*
- *On trains and buses:*
  1. Sit near/next to a woman
  2. If you can afford it, take the more expensive option as it will tend to carry a better class of person and so be more hassle free.
- *Take Tampax and contraception with you – sanitary towels are cheap and readily available, but Tampax are expensive and harder to find.*
- *Assume everyone is trying to con you – they probably are, especially in the tourist areas!*
- *Take your Walkman – on long journeys it is a great way of being in your own world, but it also means that people can't engage you in conversation.*

Cathy's Top, Top, Tip!

If someone tries to touch you up in the street, don't be afraid of making a fuss, especially if you get your arse pinched, etc. Accidents do happen as you do have to brush past people, so don't get paranoid. However, if they do try and take advantage, scream and shout at them. As well as feeling better yourself, they will be embarrassed and may learn that it's not acceptable.

DON'T:

- Show any bare flesh – except the unavoid-able. Whatever the weather cover shoulders, legs, stomach and chest.

- Wear tight clothes (see Nina's comments later) as are hot plus grabbing attention.

- Attract attention with clothes or behaviour (except the last DO before)

- Make eye contact in the street.

- Eat what you consider to be dodgy meat – it's better to be safe than sorry... one way of avoiding food poisoning.

- Forget that countries such as the Middle East are known for their hospitality, ie by being totally paranoid you may miss out or offend. Use your judgement.

- Put your camera or wallet/purse on show. Keep them secure and hidden.

- Rely totally on guide books. They are good for guidance, but are quickly out of date.

What are work opportunities like?

Well would I surprise you if I said that work opportunities for female back-packers are a lot better than for us men... or am I just being a jealous male chauvinist! I don't hear any moans of sympathy out there, but then we prob-ably don't deserve it anyway! Always ask at hostels, very good/sought after jobs, great if you can get them. Agencies are always a good bet if you intend to stay in a place for a while. Telesales are mundane but can pay well. Avoid door to door, as you'll usually get ripped off. Australia is one of the best places to find work.

Australia

Are you going to Australia? It has excellent medical care via "Medicare". It is good for things like smear tests, as they test once a year there... so use it. Get a Medicare card on arrival. When I had the stitches put in my head it cost a fair bit. Without a Medicare card I had to wait until my claim went through the system. Similarly, if you have a working visa, ensure you get your 'tax file number' early, otherwise they can do you for a lot of tax, which is very difficult to get back. If you're working for money at that point, the last thing you'll want to do is wait six months to get it all back.

Blend in

If you do this at all times you won't stick out from the crowd, and you'll be fine.

Last words from Jane

"I realised that there was much much more to life than work and Britain. Since returning I don't believe that anything in life will be as exciting as travelling was. Every bad day I have I just want to pack my bags and go. Over the 18 months I was safe, and very rarely felt unsafe or at risk. Nothing was stolen or lost, and I wasn't frightened by being a solo traveller. Final tip… You meet lots of horny men, just don't snog them all. You'll be surprised just how a reputation can travel up the East Coast in Australia."

Tom to finish

Up the East Coast of Australia and across to South East Asia are the words that I think Jane is fumbling for! **Common sense, patience, good humour, and a 6th sense that you'll develop along the way will be your most valuable assets.** These will look after you and provide you with the travel experience of a lifetime. Now, what are you waiting for?

You know you can do it, so go and do it!

Good Luck

TOP TIP!

If travelling alone, try and choose loose comfortable clothes. Apart from the practicality of it, it avoids outlining your body, and so also avoids unwanted male attention… which I'm lead to believe "can be more than a little boring" according to Nina… she must have met a few of my mates!

CHAPTER 8

Going with a friend

'A pleasant companion reduces the length of the journey.'
Publilius Syrus 50 BC
... *an unpleasant one just annoys the shit out of you!!*

This is quite easily the most preferred way of travelling... a couple of friends from school or college decide that it's about time they went off to see the big wide world. You've talked about it a lot, dreamt about it, and the time is getting near. The best thing about travelling with a friend is that you really do motivate each other, which is a very good thing. You may well have been in the situation where countless other friends have stated an intention of coming with you, even a few... 'yeah, of course I'm definitely coming', and others who have talked about going off to see other parts of the world with other friends of yours. But in the end of the day you know that they are only being the impotent parrot... 'all talk and no action!'

Again we're back on to my brother Mat's wise old saying about the '**doers**' and '**talkers**' in this world... these kind of people are 'talkers' and will spend their life 'talking' about all these fantastic things that they are going to do. And then in 30 years time they will be the ones that rabbit on to people like us about the things they have always wanted to do, but never quite did for some reason or another... for which they'll have an adequate number of excuses. But inside I'm sure they'll really feel that they missed out on this opportunity in life... one which you're about to take!

☛ *OK, so we've established that you and your friend(s) are 'doers' and that you are about to do something a little bit more adventurous than a two week piss up in Corfu with the lads/lassies.*

If one, or both of you, are very nervous about doing the trip, I think you'll find that the determination of not letting your partner down will weigh quite heavily on your mind, to the extent that you will both get organised, earn the money, and go. For myself and Tony, we bought the ticket early (which we found was great for our motivation), and then worked our botties off to earn the money so as to not let the other down... he sold his nuts and his pride and joy (chestnuts and his VW Beetle that is!) and I ate 7 months worth of Big Macs, chicken burgers, fries and doughnuts on my breaks at Maccy D's.

What do we think of this then?

Well, because you're doing the trip together, really make it a trip together, i.e. don't let one of you do all the legwork because he/she is better at finding deals/maths/talking to people/shopping, etc. If you do it all together you will both know exactly what is going on, and so feel in control. This will save hassles later on, especially with situations like... 'well you're the one who persuaded the travel agent to send us to Baghdad!'. Between you you'll be able to reach some sort of compromise as to where you'd like to visit, what you'd like to do, etc. You'll no doubt find that you'll agree on everything anyway, especially if it's been the topic of conversation for a while. However do take a bit of time between you at this stage, all the more so if there are more than two of you travelling together.

If you've read Decisions already, you'll know what I'm talking about. So time to jump in with:

TOP TIP!

Get to the travel agents and thrash out some ideas. If you are the one who is doing less of the talking because you feel happy to do what the others want to do, don't! Remember that it is your trip too, so make sure you have your say and then work out some sort of compromise, as you'll only regret it later... something that you obviously don't want.

Is (are) your companion(s) the right choice?

Have you even thought about this? Many don't as you tend to think, 'Well they've been my friend for quite a few years now.' But... is there something about them that annoys you intensely? Remember that you're about to spend virtually 24 hours a day travelling with them for however many months. There is a saying that 'You really don't know someone unless you've lived with them!' Well I've just thought of a similar one...

'You really don't know how annoying your friend's sleeptalking, fussiness, smelly feet, bad breath, drunken misbehaviour, major untidiness/picky tidiness, boring stories, lousy jokes, chronic flatulance... are... until you've travelled with them!'

Looking back at that last bit... it just about sums me up. God knows how Tony put up with me!

Girlfriend/boyfriend?

I'm sorry to say that if you are planning a 'big trip' together, **beware**. I really do mean this in big neon letters, with sirens going off, and the works. If you are really keen on that person then it is a very big risk to take. The number of couples I've met, i.e., not just heard about, but **actually met,** who have broken up mid trip, has amazed me, and **actually put me off ever travelling with a girlfriend.** Mind you, if she was loaded and it was a first-class trip around the world to places I'd like to go, with all my spending/going out included... then I might be persuaded to think about relaxing this rule... but only once mind! The variations on 'going out' range from anything from a couple of months to the 'dangerously serious' couple of years. For some reason it doesn't seem to work.

BUT I'm not going to put a dampner on it too much (if I haven't already!) as I've met loads of couples who've been fine, and who've had a great time. In fact the intrepid Helena has done this a couple of times, and has the opposite view to me... so there we go. However she does reiterate the point that I made that if you are keen on the person, it is a very big risk to take. So think really carefully. So what am I trying to say?... well, I'll be totally honest with you, it is a difficult one, so I'll throw you a few little thought provokers for you to think about.

☞ *OK, so what problems are there, and why should you be careful?*

◆ It's a lot of money spent which tends to weigh heavily on your mind when you are having problems.
◆ Everyone else you meet seems to be single and having a wild time.
◆ Because of No. 2, you can be seen as 'the couple', and if you're not careful you can be left out of a few things... this may piss you off a bit, and you may then start blaming your partner for something which may not be their fault, leading to tension, and then seeing only the bad things in them!
◆ You may prefer to take a double room for more privacy; however sometimes this may not be possible, so you may find you are the only couple in a dormitory. The problems occurring in No.3 or any strains at all may well become apparent to your room mates, who although they try their best may not be too subtle about the fact that they know. This may cause you further discomfort and problems.
◆ You will be spending 24 hours a day with each other, for the whole duration of the trip. Have you ever done this before? Many couples tend to work extremely hard right up to the departure point, taking all the overtime possible to earn the money, and so hardly see each other. They then look forward to going away and spending some time with each other. Once away the first part is great, finally spending time together. However after a while the novelty wears off, it then grows tiresome, and then the problems begin.
◆ You are thousands of miles away from home, and from the support and advice of friends, forcing you to sort out your problems, or face a massive phone bill!

However, there is a famous saying, probably from some equally famous person, '**Que sera, sera**' – '**If it was meant to be, then it will be**'. I'm a firm believer in this, and I think that I shouldn't in any way be the one to discourage travelling with your partner, because it can be a very enjoyable way of seeing the world. I suppose it is also a great way of getting to know your partner better. I just want to make sure the warning signs are out there, plain to see in black and white, so that you do go away and seriously think about what you are about to do.

With a friend/some friends?

If you've read the above then you pretty much know what I am about to say. If you haven't, give it a quick once over. In fact, to be honest, not much really needs to be said. The fact that you have decided to go with these people is an indication of your like and trust them. But it is worth having a quick think, as there is always the possibility of a fall out… 'His repetitive annoying laugh', 'Her exaggerated stories', etc.

☞ *If it is an intense annoyance with one of these things, think what 24 hours a day will be like with this person… will it drive you nuts?*

Or maybe your conversation is only held together by your taste in men/women… or both! This will soon run dry, and there's nothing worse than travelling with a companion with no conversation, well… maybe a sweaty sauna with Claire Rayner… but this surely comes a close second! If you can be honest with yourself and others about this then it will be better for you in the long run, but don't be so honest so as to cause a major bust up… diplomacy is the order of the day! You'll surely regret it if this ends up ruining your trip, and if you end up going your separate ways, having had a major bust up with a good friend. It does occasionally happen.

☞ *It is definitely better to go into these things with an open mind, and with everything that really has to be said, actually said, and then forgotten about.*

Are your budgets fairly similar?

There really is nothing worse than feeling guilty about tucking in to a nice juicy bit of shark steak, or octopus, or feeling how your palate copes with the delights of crocodile accompanied by one of the local wines… as your travelling buddy tiresomely ploughs through another omelette and asks for another glass of water. You may both indicate politely to each other that you don't really mind, but it does put a bit of a dampener on the occasion! Similarly, as you fall in to your room and wake your pal up at God knows what hour, completely off your box from excessive drinking, for the 6th time that week (and it's still only Saturday!)… when he/she had to retire early as he/she couldn't afford to go to the club with the rest of you – this may settle on the nerves a bit, and start to ruin the trip a smigin. So do bear it in mind.

So… that's the general idea of the sort of ground rules you should think about making, even before you go. You should also establish who should send off for what, find out about this and that, etc. **Even write them down on the back of a beer mat (depending on how pissed you are!), signing it, then putting it away and finally forgetting about it**. It will all be said and

TOP TIP!

Making ground rules. What I'm leading up to is that it is always a good idea to establish some basic ground rules over a few beers some night... serious ones like:

1. It being OK to go your separate ways for a few days if agreed by all parties concerned, or even for good if you really don't get on. If you've caught the gist of what I've been saying so far – that travelling is easy, too easy sometimes, it is very easy to meet further up the road somewhere at a certain time. This will give you all/both a bit of time and space apart.

2. Agree to have some sort of meeting or something, some way you can air your views if you are unhappy about anything. But most importantly, always agree to find a solution i.e. not to argue about it too much, as you'll find this pointless and a waste of time. You'll soon see that arguing solves nothing when travelling with friends, although I doubt you'll ever find time or anything to argue about anyway!

Get everything said and out in the open now. Therefore it's been said, so you can now get on with the important stuff.

done, and noted in the back of your mind... for future and emergency use only! The beer mat will then be one of those momentos that you will find in a few years time, pull out, and have a laugh at. 'Those were the days, eh?'

Scouts and brownies... be prepared!

Ground rules sorted out, tickets bought, money earned, strategy worked out... you'll find your departure date will fly upon you quicker than the shits after a dodgy vindaloo! They say you should learn from your own and other people's mistakes, which I suppose is what a lot of this book is really about. So, don't go in blind, **do make sure you are prepared**... for instance make sure you can put your tent up and down and that it's all there before you leave.

☞ *So get the checklists going, and everything bought and put aside. The last thing you need is a last minute rush around (although it does get the old heart pumping!). Departure day arrives... you go... you're gone!*

The advantage of travelling with others, especially if you are a particularly nervous pair, is that you can see what you are like just by looking at the others! **You're both going through the same thing together, and you'll find that in every situation you pull each other through.** You'll soon find out all sorts of things about your companion that you never knew. Tony for example found out my love for practising my didgeridoo... early in the morning... in our two man tent! He also found out that I wasn't very good at first... was I, Tony?

Advantages

The more confident one will always be able to start conversations to get you both introduced to others. If you are a two, three or more, you will find it easy to join big groups of people, or to start your own, and so become known by people wherever you go. **Exhibitionists** – if this is one of the best words in the English dictionary to describe you... then all the better! It is very easy to 'perform' double acts at the backpacker places you go to, and so to become known and get to meet people. We have all met them, and still can remember them and their antics! If you're that kind of person, yet not too overbearing with it, you will have a lot of fun in most of the backpacker places you go to, and make a lot of great friends.

But don't go over the top, as you'll just end up looking like Victor Pratt and his Marshmallow side kick! You'll then get the opposite effect of making people want to avoid you, or attracting only fruitcakes like yourself.

☞ *You will also find travelling with a partner very useful when you need to find accommodation.*

Tony and I for example would use this to our advantage if we arrived some-where either by air, bus, or plane. One would sit looking after the bags, while the other went off in search of hotels, hostels, taxis, food, etc. This tended to work well, especially in poorer countries where you are confronted with thousands of smiley faces all promising the earth, and at a great price too (*see* **Tips** as to how to deal with these situations). The only thing you need to worry about therefore is who is trying to rip you off, and where the best place to stay really is, as you can actually go in to each place and have a look for yourself... and you don't have to worry about your belongings and the weight of them. You may well find that accommodation is cheaper if there are two of you sharing a room, and it will invariably be safer, as you may get a lockable room, as opposed to a bunk bed in a dormitory.

Budgeting

◆ If there are two of you **sharing a tent** on the odd occasion, you will find that this makes the cost of accommodation minimal. In Australia, for example, if you pitch your tent in the caravan parks you'll get the use of a pool, BarBQ, and good facilities for no more than a couple of quid each, plus the added security of your friendly neighbours watching over your tent for you (as they are usually OAP's who have retired there and who welcome the chance to help out some young Poms).

TOP TIP!

Backpackers are generally good about not nick-ing each other's food, but to be on the safe side always wrap/tie it up tightly in a couple of plastic bags, and then write your name and the date on the outside with a permanent black marker pen. Then stuff it into a cor-ner at the back of the fridge. Communal fridges tend to be fairly big. If anyone is going to whip something it will usually be from the front where it is easily accessible. But this is a minor point, so don't worry too much about it.

◆ In most parts of Africa you can just about pitch a tent anywhere, just be pre-pared to exchange food with anyone who questions your presence. Never thrust money at 'inquisitors', as you may find yourself besieged, or worse, offending someone who was just trying to be friendly.

You'll find it is always easier to budget with more than one person, as you will stop each other overspending, and you'll find that you can eat more cheaply with buying for two/three.

If you stay in a place for more than one day, do take advantage of fridges and cupboards. These will enable you to buy in advance for your stay, thus saving money by buying in bulk.

Going with a friend(s) means that you will never be lonely, and there will always be someone there in times of trouble.

Disadvantages?

Well there aren't many disadvantages, only that you'll spend virtually 24 hours a day with each other, and if you're the type of person who would be driven nuts by this… I really think that you should seriously think about it. The thing is that you're about to spend a fair amount of hard earned money, and you may well end up ruining your trip and a friendship. **There is a feeling of being obliged to each other, not letting each other down, etc.** This is only fair, as you'll probably have been good friends for a while before deciding to travel together, and so naturally won't let each other down. **This is why I really can't stress enough the importance of establishing some ground rules before you go,** as this can only be fair for you and your partner(s).

If you think that maybe you'd really like to have more freedom for a bit, why not go alone, and arrange to meet up with your friend(s) somewhere en route, maybe even agree to do the 'home leg' solo, or agree to the possibility of it happening.

But certainly agree to the possibility of making space for yourselves if you feel that you may need it, and be adult enough not to get offended by it. If you are good friends then you'll find that this is easy to do, and so should be no worries anyway.

However, I don't need to tell you this do I! Once this is out of the way you'll be so bloody excited about going that it'll all be forgotten.

Got a companion? Got a ticket? Think ya gotta go then!

CHAPTER 9

Safety

'To get attention always shout 'Fire!' instead of 'Help!'as you are guaranteed a better response'. Tom Griffiths 12.3.97 (read it somewhere, sounds good, like it!!)

This is something that I am always asked a lot of questions about, and is a fairly serious subject in that it is often one of the deciding issues as to whether a person will go travelling or not.

☞ **'Yes I know that it's probably fantastic out there, all the beaches, the sun, the fun, and all of that... but will I be safe?'.**

Many people are put off going to places like South East Asia, South America, parts of Africa, etc. Indeed some of the places are a little dangerous at times for backpackers and should be avoided for your own good. Obviously I'm talking about the places that you know to be dangerous, i.e. Rwanda, Cambodia, etc., not the places **you think** to be dangerous, but probably aren't. If you are worried about a particular country that you would like to visit, you can always ring up the Foreign Office Travel Advice number in the back of the book, and they will tell you anything that you would like to know concerning the state of the country at the time.

It's not as dangerous as you think

I know I have touched briefly on a lot of what I am about to say on this subject already throughout the book, I hope that I'm not going to repeat myself too much, but I just feel that if I get a lot of it down here in one section then you might find it all a bit easier to swallow... and I hope believe! Travelling really isn't as dangerous as you are all lead to believe nowadays. The world is scared, society is scared, everyone is scared of something. I think that this is a shame, and would've loved to have lived in the 1930's for example where people were nice to each other, children could hitch-hike, and you could leave your doors unlocked at night. Those were the days!

This is why the thought of unknown places such as South East Asia, and the scary stories that we always hear about, are enough to put even the hardiest of us out there off. Even I was a bit sceptical when I first thought of it as an option. However, **it is safe**, and it is a lot easier to travel round than you think.

What about your own personal safety?

I believe that the best thing you can go travelling with for your own safety is a bit of self confidence and common sense. When at University in Manchester loads of students got (and are still getting) mugged everyday because of their carefree 'Hey, I'm so bloody great, no one will mug me!' attitude. Just out of school, away from parents for the first time – TA TA TA TA TA TAAAAA... Captain Invincible, balls the size of King Kong's... get mugged?... **Not I!**... I'll never be mugged, that happens to other people (everything always happens to other people!). The next day, in tears on phone to mum... 'Sob Sob... the knife was huge, there were ten of them... whimper sniff... they forced me to give them all my money... I tried to fight back, in fact I did, yes I did fight back... I think I put 3 of them in hospital!'

In reality what happened was that a ten year old came up to him/her in broad daylight with a broken bottle and said 'Gis yer money or I'll slash you'. Despite the size of this little puplet you hand over all your money, and the cheeky little bugger runs off in delight. This is actually a common occurrence in the student areas of Manchester as all the students will testify. So what would you do in that instance... go on, put yourself in the student's shoes and say what you would do?

♦ Tell him to clear off back to playschool, and while he's at it run under a bus on the way home?
♦ Give him a clip round the ear, take the bottle off him, and either let him run away or hold him until the police arrive?
♦ Ignore him, and if he's not too close walk or run in the opposite direction.
♦ Say 'I wonder what that policeman over there would think if he knew what you were doing?' and while the kid is distracted, get out of there.
♦ Give him your money.

If your answer is Numbers 1. or 2. you have obviously never been mugged before and think that you are some kind of a macho idiot.

Unless you are trained to stand up to attackers, and have some kind of black belt to prove it, then this is really not a good idea. Yes you may well get a quick lucky kick or punch in, but you are severely missing the point here.

85

The point is that no matter what age, height, sex, or race the attacker is, th person (with a weapon) is still a threat. If you decide to take them on the you will end up being one of these people that gets stabbed or slashed by little kid just for the money in your pocket. They have nothing to lose, oth erwise they would be doing something else.

What about your pride though?
What about living the rest of your life with 15 stitches across your face?

Circumstances: answers 3, 4, and 5 obviously depend on the circum stances of the attack, the surroundings, etc. Obviously if you are backed int a dark corner at night you must ask yourself the question

☞ **'Is my life worth the amount of money in my pocket?'**

If you think that your life is only worth £20–£30 max., then go for it… take them on! Personally I reckon that my life is worth about the value of the UK's GDP, which is considerably more than what I will ever carry in my pocket. So what do you do?

Assess the situation

There is absolutely no shame in doing a runner from a kid with a weapon. They have nothing to lose, and in the end of the day it is very unlikely that they will ever be caught. I know of people that have been stabbed by kids as young as 8. You only have to look at the news of the past couple of weeks:

◆ A baby was stabbed whilst in a pram as the mother was being mugged
◆ A pensioner was slashed across the face by another young mugger
◆ An old lady was killed in her home during a burglary

It's a bad old world out there. Things like this happen everyday to all sorts of people. I was mugged in France, I wasn't the first and I definitely wasn't the last. If you run away from a mugger (depending on the circum stances of course) are they really going to run after you? No… they're going to get the hell out of there before the Law turns up. They're not going to run after you, tackle you to the ground, and then wrestle the money off you! However this is for you to assess, and for you to decide. I don't want any of you coming back to me saying 'Well you said do this, so I did and got hurt!' – 'cos I didn't…

☞ *in the end of the day the final decision and how you react is entirely up to you*

Put it down to experience and learn from it

It's nothing to be ashamed of; it happens everyday, but there are a few things that you can do:

- Carry 'mugger's money' around with you, a small amount of money so that if you do get mugged you hand it over straight away with the impression that it is all the money that you have.
- Make yourself less of a target, don't be conspicuous, blend in.
- Take care when walking at night, be alert and aware of your surroundings.
- Take care when walking in daylight, be alert and aware of your surroundings!

Very deliberate there... **the point that I have made previously in the book is that you are more likely to be mugged in your own town than in somewhere like Delhi, Mexico City, New York, etc.** This is simply because you are more aware of your surroundings in unfamiliar territory. In your own town you are not aware simply because you see the same things around you everyday. There do seem to be more muggings in broad daylight, maybe because you are less suspecting, whereas people generally make themselves less of a target now at night. That's only my theory... but it's a thought, and backs up what I'm saying quite well.

- Stay calm, because if you panic they might panic.
- If you're not Jean Claude Van Dam, make out that you're Elmer Fudd, they may then underestimate you.
- Trouble in a bar/in the street... if it's got nothing to do with you, stay away, don't get involved (obviously depending on the circumstances). There is always someone bigger and harder than you out there. In Asia for example, they may be only 4'2", but they may be deadly at kickboxing!
- When travelling you are number 1, you are the priority here... look after yourself and others with you. Avoid trouble, and avoid others who invite trouble.
- Running to safety is not cowardice, it's common sense... especially when you are miles from home, can't speak the language, and can easily be framed by a local with a bit of collaboration if they have something against you. In times like these, don't faff around, get in touch with the Embassy asap.

Don't be flashy, be safe

- Be careful about flashing valuables around, even amongst fellow backpackers. Yup, I'm sorry to say it but you do get one or two arseholes, or the odd local 'infiltrator'.

◆   Hotel/hostel safes: do you consider them to be safe?

◆   Be careful about leaving things near open (or even closed for that matter) windows, especially if on street level or next to a fire escape, as thieves can easily reach in.

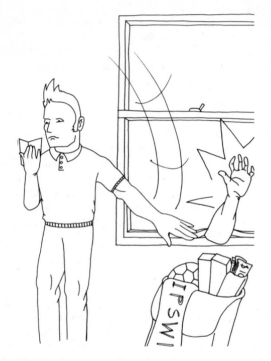

◆   Make sure you do take little padlocks and chains. You'll then be able to chain your belongings to the bed, seats in airports/buses/trains, etc. However if a thief really wants to get into your stuff they will – with a knife! They are therefore there as a deterrent and for security, as the bag cannot simply be whipped from where it is. So don't go overboard with the padlocks and chain, they just need to be visible. If you lose your keys to them they should be small/weak enough that you can break them yourself to get in.

◆   Make sure the locks work on the door and that there is some kind of emergency exit out of the building. Remember that if you don't like the room, ask for a better one, after all you are the one paying for it.

◆   Be careful who you give your address to, or where you are staying before you have worked out their intentions.

TOP TIP!

Remove the airline/bus baggage identification labels as it points to the fact that you are a tourist and where you come from. Mind you, humping a bloody great backpack on your back does nothing for your disguise as 'Jo Local' and tends to give the game away somewhat – but I think you realise what I am getting at!! Do keep some identification somewhere permanently in your backpack so that if it does get mislaid somewhere it will come back 'Return to Sender'. Also be aware of any other identifying marks on your luggage that can tell anyone anything about you. Good con men may use this as an opportunity to start up a conversation: 'Have you been to Australia yet? I stayed at a great place called Geoff's Place on Magnetic Island (having seen some sort of sticker/label on your baggage with Geoff's Place on). You may think that he's a top bloke, he's not, he's just clever, and will just bull shit, work your conversation, build up your trust, all with the intention of robbing you later.

Again I can't stress enough how rare something like this is, but I feel that if I play on your paranoia enough in your head you will look out for yourself and be aware and ready for anything...

Why is this guy being really friendly to me? What are his intentions? How does he know that I am British? How does he know that I have just been to Fiji? Why is he looking at my stuff? What does he want?

A little bit of suspicion will look after you and help you develop that sixth sense of yours. If they are worth trusting they will gain your trust in the usual ways.

Trouble/Thieves

◆ There probably aren't as many out there as it might seem – the horror stories that you hear have been exaggerated about 100x by the time that they reach you.

◆ Never risk a fight unless you have served in the SAS for at least 3 years, and even then, be cautious!

◆ Don't look as though you are about to go for your gun!
◆ Whatever the situation is, it will all be over in a couple of seconds and you'll never see that person again… so put it down to experience and get on with your life.
◆ If your bag is snatched do think about giving chase (if they had the guts for a confrontation they would do it in the first place); they may well drop it due to the weight and you in pursuit.

However

◆ Don't get yourself into hotter water than you already are by running into dark/quiet areas or getting lost.
◆ Make sure all of your valuables are in your day bag, and get used to not letting this out of your sight (so if your pack does get nicked at least you'll have the money to buy a new one + clothes, etc.)
◆ If you look after your things properly, this will never happen (**it is very very very rare as it is anyway**). The thing is, with all of your belongings in this little pack, you tend to look after it extremely well anyway… **So don't worry too much!**

TOP TIP!

Why not take a quick self defence course before you go. They are available everywhere, and do wonders for your self confidence. I know I have mentioned this in the 'Tips' as well, it's just that I think it's so important that if I mention it twice you might take it in… I'm not just being a dozy pratt!

☞ *In the end of the day, don't have nightmares!*

As I've hinted all the way through this book, once you are on the backpacker trail you will find that you are mixing with people like yourself, and you will be perfectly safe. I am assuming that you all have a bit of common sense about you, and that you will learn pretty quickly how to suss people out, look after yourself, and generally become a little bit 'streetwise'. People are always joking about this expression, but we all have to learn it.

I learnt it on my first trip. You've got to realise that I was brought up in the country, schooled in the town, but still had quite a 'quiet' childhood. As far as I was concerned 'grass' was what I used to cut in the garden with the lawnmower, 'smack' was what I used to get on my bum when I did anything

wrong, 'gear' was one of the things in a car that made it go, and 'acid' was what I used to add to various rocks in my chemistry lessons to make them 'fizz'. As for 9-year-olds with broken bottles, con men with no teeth, and strangers nicking my things if I left them out in the open and turned my back... *naart in Straaatford St. Maaary boiy... naaart in moiy vyllige... cos oim a caaantry boiy aaarnt oi !*

We all make mistakes, and we all learn by them. It's just that on a big trip you are exposed to more things that test you than you could possibly imagine. If you are aware and ready for whatever travelling can throw at you, then you will have no troubles.

☞ *Travelling is easy and it is not as dangerous as it is made out to be. Being confident and 'streetwise' is something that you will learn, as it is not available in the shops.*

☞ *Assess each situation as it happens, keep calm, and use your judgement to make what you consider to be a rational decision. If you aim to be safe... you will be.*

CHAPTER 10

Money and Finances

'Getting money is like digging with a needle; spending it is like water soaking into sand.' Japanese Proverb.

How much does it cost?

One of the biggest questions that I am always asked is, '**How much did it cost, what did you spend, how did you budget your trip?**' If I gave an answer it would only be a rough estimate as to how much my account had increased into the red, or by what my bank manageress (I must point out again what a fantastic lady she really is, extending my student overdraft in times of need, to pay for a flight here, and a ticket there... the 'listening bank'!) has let me have.

But as you realise, unfortunately the hard part about this financing stuff is that you are simply going to have to sit down and work out what is really viable.

I know it's not what you want to hear, but that is the nasty truth, but also the 'fun' of it, if I'm allowed to use that word! Once you know roughly how much your ticket and insurance is going to cost, you will have to work out your earning potential, savings, and what you'll need to buy before you go. Once you've done this you'll realise that unless you've got a fantastic inheritance to dig into, or the trip is to be a present, you're going to have to start saving **now**! This is why I've tried to get you as many money saving vouchers as I can, because you'll find that every penny will start to count.

However, as I hope you will also realise, the whole part of working to earn the money to do this trip is all part of the 'year off experience'. Once you've done it you will find it incredibly satisfying to know that you are going to be rewarded for everything you have done in such a great way. For me, this plays a major part in the whole result of what you achieve at the end of a year abroad… everything you did was achieved because of **your efforts**, and no-one else's but you. Makes you feel kind of good inside, probably the first major thing you have ever achieved in your life?… it was for me!

How to earn the money?

If you don't have it, and you want to travel let's say in January, don't hang around… get a job! Many will laugh on hearing me say that, in that I haven't (compared to most of my friends) held down many jobs. However when I have needed to work, I have worked extremely hard, i.e. all the overtime possible. I have also held up to three jobs at a time. For many this is the real decider in the question of will I/won't I go, as they may have to put it off due to lack of money. Either they haven't theoretically had the capacity to earn the money, or they haven't had the real desire to go anyway.

☞ *My theory is that if you really want to go, and if you have the capacity to earn the money, then there is no real reason why it shouldn't happen.*

After all, for myself, the motivation has always been there in that I have always wanted to go. As long as I budget well enough, every £10 that I earn will support me for one to two days away in a foreign country.

☞ *With this kind of motivation it is hard to justify a smoking habit that costs about £20 a week, or going out and drinking away another £30/40 a week.*

If you hear yourself saying ' £20… and the rest Tom!' then you really should think about some serious budgeting. OK, so leaving in January for example school or college finishes in June/July, which gives you about six months to earn a bit of money. If we base this on about £100 a week, which to a lot of you if you are working loads of overtime, will be underestimated anyway... you'll gross about £2400... *minimum*!

How to help keep this figure up as high as possible?

Well, live at home always seems to be the best option, because unless you're earning a fantastically high wage, by the time you've paid

- ◆ your rent
- ◆ all the bills (gas, water, electricity and phone)
- ◆ and all your other living expenses

... you're going to take forever to save all that money! By living with your parents you'll be able to negotiate a minimum rent (always use the threat of living with them until you are 40... seems to work!), or in fact pay no rent at all, which is even better! Parents will try any old trick to get rid of their offspring nowadays!.

So with any luck you'll have

- ◆ free board
- ◆ a fridge always stocked up with food
- ◆ a job with loads of money coming in
- ◆ a goal to aim at
- ◆ and sweet dreams of far away places!

Nevertheless it is always nice to contribute in some way to your parents, so they don't actually feel like a hotel, and may actually be sad when you go... and I suppose be there when you get back (you never know, they might well move whilst you're away, and not leave a forwarding address – so don't piss them off!)

Tax

- ◆ **If you're not obliged to pay it, make sure you don't.** You may well be told that you will get a refund at the end of the tax year, i.e. in April (as it runs from April to April). Fantastic you may think, but don't be fobbed off by this, as this money is no good to you if you are halfway around the world by that time! If you are earning money for travel, make sure you get it all before the plane takes off.

- ◆ **If you are a full-time student** you will find that you are not liable for tax, and should sign the appropriate tax redemption form (P32). If you are going to earn less than the limit (at the time of writing this was about

£3500), you will not be taxed either. You will only pay National Insurance Contributions which are fairly minimal anyway.

◆ **If you are taxed you must get your employer to sort out the correct tax code for you.** You should then be refunded what has been taken off, and so given back what is due to you. If you end up returning from your trip to find a refund from the Inland Revenue of £50 waiting for you, it may well be a bonus to buy some beer or new clothes, but you will regret how far that money could have got you in Asia, South America or Africa for example. A long way! You'll probably use it to pay off some debt or other. If you've earned it, I say... use it!

◆ **If you have to pay tax,** then I do apologise for harking on at the wonders of not paying it, and I wish you luck in saving the money to travel.

Local currency

Getting ripped off when changing money nowadays is very rare, especially with those friends of yours Thomas Cook, American Express (AMEX), and your 'flexible friends'. Years of experience of people getting ripped off with money has created a very strong and safe system for carrying money around the world. In fact (as I shall elaborate on later on), AMEX are extremely efficient if things go wrong, and also offer its fantastic postal system for all of its customers... wherever you are in the world.

TOP TIP!

It is always sensible to arrive in the country with a small amount of the local currency if possible (£20+). This will save you the hassle of trying to find a local currency exchange, and will possibly save you money with the airport/hotel commission charges. It may also save you getting ripped off by a local 'currency exchange' as soon as you arrive before you realise that your pound will in fact actually get you 5,000 blags, instead of the 500 you got from the one eyed 'currency man' in the street who swore that he'd met Princess Diana, and had amazingly been to where you live in England on his last visit there! Unfortunately for you it was late, you had no money for a taxi, and so you had to swallow your scepticism and take his word for it!

Changing money

Like everything nowadays, shop around. Back at home, before you go, weigh up the banks and their rivals.

◆ **Ask your bank what's the best deal that it can do for you**. Mine for example (at the time of writing) gives me free travellers cheques with my student account, and will change the money back free of charge. When changing into foreign money, again it will charge no commission. And to be totally honest, that is perfectly all right with me!

◆ If you know when you are going to leave the country, **why not ask them if it is worth buying your currency now or later**... as they'll be able to tell you if it is appreciating or depreciating at the time. On the eve of your departure it may be worth jotting down what the currencies are worth over here for all the countries you are going to, so that when you arrive you will have some sort of idea.

◆ **When you land in these places miles away from the comfort of your local high street, the same rule applies**... shop around! You have the time to do so, so you might as well use it to try and save yourself some money.

◆ **If changing small amounts, check the commission**. The rate may be good, but the company may take a percentage above a certain figure, and a fixed amount below. There are always many companies who will change money. In developed countries you will have no problems, but beware in less developed countries, as these guys will rip you off if you don't treat them confidently enough.

◆ **If you think they are in the process of ripping you off**, quote to them what you think is a better deal, and then **walk out** if they say no… you can always return if you can't get a better deal elsewhere.

◆ The other option you'll find yourself being offered in many of the poorer countries, is the **black market**… you do get a good rate, but it is illegal. When approaching this question, Colin came up with a great way of looking at it… the country is your host, so don't shit on the carpet. But again, circumstance will usually determine what you will do, just be fully aware of what you are letting yourselves in to, and aware of the consequences… as well as being illegal, in many places it is used as a ploy to target a mugging victim (as they know exactly how much money you have!).

Handling cash

Do be aware at all times when dealing with your money out in the open. Is there anyone watching you? When handling large amounts of money, there is a temptation to count it there and then. The best advice is to try and handle it as though there is very little money there anyway, maybe only one or two notes instead of ten (a handy skill to have). To be honest this doesn't really need to be said, as the declining safety on our own streets gives you more than enough practice to deal with handling money in the darkest streets of India! Are you really going to get money out at night, or in isolated places?

Didn't think so.

Credit cards

If you have access to them, they are a very good idea to have or to get hold of. **The advantage of them is that you have instant access to a large amount of money that will get you out of any situation, and back home if need be**. However they do need a lot of careful looking after (*see* Credit cards '**Tips**') as the amount of forgery that can be done with them nowadays is incredible, leaving you to foot the bill when you return. The legitimate bill will also be there when you return, so again there is the problem of overspending.

Been there, done that! I thought that if I only used it in 'emergencies' then I would be OK. Unfortunately when you're away for a long period of time it is very easy to clock up a big bill without realising it… a bit here, a present there, bungy jump, rafting, etc., etc. There is also the temptation to stick it in a cash machine to get out a few 'readies'. As Claire found out in Germany a few weeks ago... it's easy to do, especially when you don't realise that you're being charged a pound each time you use it! On the other hand if you're getting out large sums of money, then a pound is a very small commission to pay.

Advantages and disadvantages but...

◆ For peace of mind, definitely worth having.

◆ It is even better if you can work out an agreement with your parents/a trusted friend to pay the bills off when they come in, so that you don't have to pay the monstrous interest rates charged when you finally get home.

◆ Some people do travel with their parent's credit cards, so if there are any problems they can get home asap.

◆ If you don't have one, but would like one, the bank may well be able to arrange it by holding your parents account as collateral... if your parents agree to it that is!

◆ Did you also know that if you are a student, many credit card companies do not charge you the annual fee for the card? Isn't being a student great... I miss it already!

International Debit Cards

This is something that I haven't used (honesty is always the best policy!) as it has only come in over the past few years, and to be truthful, I've never really seen it advertised. However, during the past couple of trips, it has surfaced as something used by loads of people, and I am always assured by them that it works. So not wanting to lead you down a blind ally, I went to the banks to investigate.

What is it then?

Basically it's your normal cash/switch card that you use over here, except that they paint a couple of extra logos on it, and it suddenly becomes a cash/switch card that you can use over there i.e. overseas. The logos are simply the Cirrus, Maestro, and Visa signs (depending of course on which bank you have and which systems they are linked to). *Simple to use?... YES!*

So why haven't I used it before? God knows! Looks like I've missed out here, but I won't in the future.

How to use it

◆ Go to any bank machine overseas and look at the choice of logos.

- If your logos match (Visa, Cirrus, etc.), you can use the machine to withdraw money in the local currency.
- If you are in a shop overseas and you spot the Maestro logo (or whatever your corresponding one is for your bank), you can use your card as a switch card.
- Basically with both of the above methods, it will only work if you have money in your account at home, as it debits it straight out.

International Debit Cards are free

All you have to do is ask at the bank and allow time for them to replace your card, and they simply change your existing card for one of these (depending on if you are eligible with the type of account that you have).

Some important points however

- Everytime you use your International Debit Card you'll pay 2% or a minimum charge of £1 (at the time of writing). Therefore, on anything up to £50 you 'theoretically' lose money, so don't take small amounts out... if travelling with friends, why not take out the first £50 – £100 worth, and then they reciprocate it somewhere down the line?
- If you think about it (carrying on from the last point) it is a great way to change money as you are paying a very small commission, and you are getting the 'competitive' rate of exchange at the time.
- Ensure your card is in good condition before you go; if not, swap it for a new one (free to do so), so you don't have the hassles of it not being able to swipe/be read.
- Don't lose your card. Oh yeah, great bit of advice Tom! But it is a serious point. These cards have to be dealt with back in the UK, which doesn't help if you're stuck out in the middle of Peru and are worrying about paying for the donkey trek you've just endured! Another good reason for you to sign over your account to a responsible person back in the UK (preferably parents), as if problems like this happen, they can easily be sorted out for you.

Travellers cheques

Thomas Cook, American Express (AMEX) or Visa? Well, again I really can't tell you which is the best, something you'll have to look into to see which more suits your needs. I have always used Mr. Cook, and he has always done me very well. Being a student the travellers cheques are free anyway through your bank and, as said above, you can always change back what you don't use free of charge. I know that at the moment, even if you aren't a student, a few places such as Thomas Cook will refund your unwanted cheques at face value without any charge, so maybe this is the direction they are going in anyway.

But of course I am saying this on the assumption that when you return you will have some money to change back. Get real Tom! **We all know that we come back totally skint having either:**
a) run out of money 2 days before, and lived off virtually nothing, with the hope that the food on the plane will bring you round and make you look not quite as hungry as you really are when you meet your parents at the airport. And anyway, the reason that you ran out of money is because you suddenly realised that you hadn't bought your mum anything, and that she might possibly kill you if you dare to return empty handed… as you get your excuses together as to just why only one of their postcards had come (the one you sent the day after you left the UK!) OR
b) realised that you are going home, and that what you have left in your pocket will only convert back to about £6.50. However, in terms of the 'tuk' currency of the back of beyond or wherever you are, that money makes you a virtual millionaire. You therefore get totally ratted, and blow the lot! However, this somewhat deviates from the subject of travellers cheques…

Advantages

♦ Well **they are very safe** for a start, which is what you really must consider as your main priority if travelling big distances with a large amount of money.

♦ They are also **fairly easy and quick to replace,** as long as you keep the carbon separate, and the other copies with a trusted friend. If this means your family, all the better.

♦ AMEX travellers cheques also **offer other advantages** as well as being useful and reliable – such as the postal service where they will hold post for you for 3 months.

I must admit though, after seeing the advert quite recently for AMEX, about the guy who had his holiday saved because of owning American Express, I was quite sceptical. However since talking to Helena about them, my attitude has changed. Whilst in Lima, Peru, she was conned out of her cheques. When she went to American Express for help, she got £500 immediate compensation, AND some mail that was waiting for her from one of her friends. Bargain!

♦ **If you take them in a strong currency**, such as American dollars (not always best to take good old British £££££'s) **you should be able to maintain the value of your money wherever you go in the world**. This is something you should discuss with someone at your bank well before you go. Find out what they advise you to take. If they do advise you to take dollars for example, and you know that you are getting a lot of dollars to the pound at the moment, watch to see what they do. If it starts to fall, maybe you should think about buying. If it continues to rise right up to the day of your departure, all the better for you! The thing is, if you are changing a lot of money, these little changes may make a bit of difference. It might not, but at the end of the day, as long as you don't feel that you have missed out, then you will go away happy.

Disadvantages

Not many really. The only thing that you have to watch out for is that you don't pay too much commission.

◆ You often get lower rates than for cash.
◆ If countersigned they are useless. Therefore don't start to countersign until you are absolutely positive that you are about to change them for cash. If you change your mind... you can't, as other places won't accept them if not signed in front of them.
◆ Beware of the **'fixed rate'** or **'percentage'** words on their signs. Sometimes if you are only changing a small amount you may be charged a fixed amount and so theoretically lose out. Usually changing large amounts means that you don't lose out too much on the conversion. Is this making any sense to you? Even I struggle, and I'm meant to be an Economist!

In short, if there are a few of you, it is always best to combine if possible to change money. If you can't and you're not sure if you are going to lose out on a lot, ask the cashier to write it all down for you... 'if I give you this, how much do I get back... how much!' (Remember that in some countries you will experience that millionaire feeling for a minute as you are given 25.4 million tuks, all in huge notes. It is at this point that if you are not fully aware of it all that you may get ripped off.)

◆ You will be told by the lovely lady at Thomas Cook (for example) that they have branches all over the world, and that if you go to them, you won't be charged commission for changing them. Very true, this happens. The only problem is arriving in New York or Delhi with only an address. They can be very difficult to find, and it can often be worth giving up a small bit of commission to save you long walks, bus rides, and getting lost.

Again though, you'll soon get into the swing of changing money. Just take your time. If like me you are hopeless with figures, write it all down, and find out just what you are paying out, and to whom. Banks are safe. As for private money changers, usually if they ask for your passport number to write on the back... bingo! they're OK. If after you have handed over the money they jump on the back of a motorbike and roar off into the distance, you may get the feeling that perhaps all is not well!

TOP TIP!

Keep the travellers cheques numbers separate, and then cross them off when you use them.

Ask at the bank when you order your cheques for small denominations. If you get stuck with large denominations such as $50 cheques you might find them difficult to change. The other problem is that it might give you too much money, forcing you to change it back into another currency and so losing out again on the commission.

However the main problem I've found with this is that if you have a large number of low/similar denominations, you'll find yourself with a whole wad of $20 cheques that is impossible to keep track of. You are therefore unsure of how many you have used, or if any have decided to go walkabout by themselves! Crossing the numbers off, writing down the number of the last cheque used, or simply writing down the number of cheques that you have left, should keep you on top of it all.

Final words… travellers cheques are good, reliable and safe. They also seem to be getting better and better all the time. I will always use them, so draw your own conclusions!

Money Transfer

What????? Something you've never heard of maybe? Well, I hadn't got a clue about it before I used it on my first big trip, and it is something that we found extremely useful. **What is it?**

Well as it says really. All the major banks in this country are affiliated/have links with major banks in other countries. If you intend to stay for a large part of your trip in one country on the other side of the world, you can transfer money to an account over there.

I'll give you my example to explain better.

I banked and still do (bless them!) with the Midland Bank. Tony and I, as you will already know, intended to spend most of our trip out in Australia, maybe even to work there. We therefore worked out roughly how much money we were going to budget ourselves out there, and arranged for the Midland to transfer the money out to the Westpac Bank in Australia. We paid a transfer fee of course, but found this to be less than the amount we would spend each time we had to change money. Once we arrived in Sydney, Australia, we went to the main Westpac Bank where our money had been sent. Within half an hour we had an Australian bank account, and a cash card with a pin number. This meant no worries about carrying the money around, as they had banks all the way up the East Coast of Australia with the trusty 'holes in the wall', and we earned interest as well. As for getting a job, the wages were paid straight in with no hassles of opening temporary accounts (difficult to do if you are a tourist with all your money tied up in travellers cheques, etc., leaving you only small amounts of money to deposit there... loads of forms to fill in!).

In terms of budgeting we thought it was great
◆ It meant that we knew exactly how much we could spend before we got there
◆ We couldn't spend any of the money until we got there
◆ And of course we knew how much we had to play with after arriving.

For ease, and just general peace of mind, I'd recommend it to anyone. Just think of all that time you won't spend queuing to change your money, and all the big notes you won't have to get out and look after. Simply step up to the hole in the wall and Bob is your Uncle!

What if I wait until I get there?
Well, in theory, this is what the money transfer is best used for. Having signed your account over to your parents, you can wait until you get to whatever country you want before asking for your money to be sent to you. If in Westernised countries you can just about do it with any bank. However, in poorer countries, you are best to go to the major banks in the capital cities.

How do I go about it?
◆ Ask the foreign bank if it will accept funds (if in a country where you don't speak the language it might be worth asking the Embassy for their help to stop any expensive cock-ups).
◆ If they do, find out their address, branch, and full bank code.
◆ Then simply ring home with the details.

◆   Get them to ring you with confirmation that it has been sent.
◆   After the alloted time period go in with full ID and withdraw the cash.

☞   *If you need the money quickly, then use the Western Union Money Transfer (outlined later on in this chapter)*

Points to note about Money Transfer (up to date at time of writing)

◆   All the major banks offer this service which is virtually identical, i.e. in the fees that you pay, speed, etc.
◆   Only some banks will offer the service to people who have their accounts in other banks, but I should imagine that you will do it through your own bank, so who cares, eh?
◆   If the money sits in the foreign account for too long it might get sent back. So make sure you get your timings right. Dare I say it – another good reason for signing your account over to your parents!
◆   Fees have to be paid at both ends. This can either be done both at this end, at either end, or pay both at that end. Do be careful if both fees are paid at this end (keep proof) so that you are not charged again.
◆   I talked above about opening up a bank account abroad. This was easier for me possibly due to the fact that I had a relative in Australia. Good old Aunty Nicky… ended up being put down as my sponsor on a whole host of forms that she didn't know about! Sponsors are great, just as long as you have their permission… cos not everyone is as trustworthy as me!

◆ Another important point about bank accounts in Australia is that there is a 'Whisper in the Wind' that some of the Australian banks are cutting down on giving bank accounts to non-residents who are there for less than a year. Having poked my nose about and asked a few awkward questions here and there, all I got was a load of jumbled replies, yes'es and no's. So all I can conclude is that maybe something like this is about to happen.

Disadvantages?

There are always some, but these only really reflect on you.

◆ **You do really have to budget until you can reach this lump sum of money**. But is this really a bad thing?
◆ **If you get a foreign bank account, it can be too easy to use the bank card in the machines and so spend loads of money.** If you can control it, it can be a very useful aid to your budgeting. If not, you could end up spending freely, too quick, and then feeling miserable because, well... because you can't really survive without any money!

In my opinion the Pro's beat the Con's on this one, so I'll leave it up to you to decide.

EMERGENCY MONEY TRANSFER

Western Union Money Transfer:
'The fastest way to send money world-wide'... and apparently it really is!
These guys have been around and doing this since 1871, perform about 30 million transfers a year, and are actually backed by the Foreign and Commonwealth Office. As they say themselves, they are 'fast, reliable, easy and convenient', and come highly recommended. Well, I suppose that if the boys in the capital are willing to back them, then they should really get the big 'thumbs up' from the young man in Suffolk. They do! In fact I'm going to make a definite plump for these boys, and give them the big green light:

☛ *If you want to get money out to you in a hurry... Use them!*

How does it work?

Well it's actually dead simple. If for example you need extra finances for whatever reason and your parents (bless them!) agree to all your demands:

◆ All they have to do is ring 0800 833 833 (or whatever the number is in the country that the sender is at the time). They will then be guided to the near-

105

est of the 28,000 agent locations worldwide... making it possible for your dad to do it even if overseas on business.

◆ The sender then takes the money to the agent, fills out a form, pays the service fee and receives a receipt with a Control Number. Your dad will then inform you of the transfer.

◆ You will then head off to your nearest agent, provide identification and then pick up the money.

If you prefer you can secure the transfer by putting in an identification, such as a question like your Mum's maiden name, granny's dog's name, or asked to name the greatest football team that has ever graced this planet... to which of course you would say 'Ipswich Town Football Club... the greatest football team to ever grace this planet!'

It really is as simple as that!

◆ All operators speak English (as well as their national language), and it is all done by computer systems so that the money can literally be sent and picked up in minutes.

◆ Furthermore most of the agents are in places which are either open 24 hours, or at any rate later than the usual 9–5 Monday – Friday, so you are even less restricted on your access to the system.

◆ The money will be converted immediately at the rate of the moment, the rates of which are very competitive, so you won't have to worry about converting it all into the local currency.

☛ ***NB Even though I have written this down under the heading of 'emergency money transfer', you may well find that for your own preference, ease, and piece of mind that this may be the best way for you to handle your finances. It is a very reliable and proven system, and so it should definitely be considered. Leave a large amount of money with your parents to be forwarded to you when you get to the other side of the world... helps you to budget no end!***

Parents

So important that I've written a full chapter on them! However in this case they can be very useful to help you with your finances.

◆ Free board before you go, if lucky.
◆ Fridge full of food!

Don't knock these until you've missed them! Those of you who have will appreciate just what I mean by this. However it is always nice to contribute to both of these… it may make them a bit more responsive to those pleas for cash later on!

TOP TIP!

For your ease you might well think of signing your bank account over to one of them, or a trusted friend. If there are any problems whilst you are away they can be dealt with immediately, rather than left to fester and get worse. These things won't go away just because you have, and they'll make a lovely nightmare end to your trip. Get them sorted at the time… by your parents. Easy, eh?

While we're on the subject of making life easy for yourself, pick the right time and see if they'll pay your credit card bill for you whilst you're away. The right time? Well I find this to be that point just after they have sat down after a three course meal… cooked by you… and washed up by you, and whilst they are contemplating just how wonderful you are, having washed the car, fed, washed and walked the dog, painted the house, paid the mortgage off, etc. You know the sort of thing.

Do not try the blackmail of threatening to leave home, as, considering your impending trip/behaviour during your teen years, they may not give a toss… leaving you homeless. Having them help you out if possible will mean that you will not find huge interest rate charges when you get home, and you can pay it off with a clear conscience. Also the threats from home whilst you are travelling about no longer paying them off will help you to budget with ease!

Carrying money

On the market there are various goods which can be bought to carry money – money belts, neck wallets, wrist wallets, or just the good old fashioned pocket.

For myself, and many others, I use a money belt, which I use to hold my passport, travellers cheques, documents, licences, etc. However I tend not to wear it as it can get itchy and sweaty. It can also be a bit of a pain in the arse if it is full of things, as it tends to get too bulky. It is often advertised a that sneaky little item that you can hide away under your clothing. Very true and on the odd occasion you will do this as the best way of hiding your valuables. However when walking in the street, it will

a) make you look fat/pregnant

b) rub against your skin and make you sweat/itch.

Many people therefore use them more as an open wallet, where you can wrap the straps around your hand (so that it can't be snatched) and then just carry it around by hand. This way you will get in the habit of carrying it with you at all times, or knowing exactly where it is, and that it is safe at all times. It is also useful to have all your important documents in it, as they can be easily obtained whenever necessary from your day bag. They'll never get lost, and you know that you'll never leave them behind.

I do also carry a wallet with all my everyday bits and pieces in, such as cash, cards, ID, etc. I carry this in my pocket, and just walk along with my hands on it when I sense that there may be pick-pockets around in crowded areas.

Locals

♦ From all of this you may now be worried that wherever you go, locals are going to try and steal from you! This is certainly not the case, as there are not as many thieves around as you think.

♦ In a country where you don't know the people or the surroundings, you may tend to think that everyone is trying to rip you off. **However this is just your natural 'survival instinct' making you paranoid to keep you alert**. This will tend to lessen the longer you travel.

♦ How I like to look at it is if you think of a foreigner in your home country walking down your high street... would your mum/dad/brother/sister rip them off? I hope not!

I can hear many of you thinking... well, maybe, Tom, but they won't be as visible as I would with a backpack and a map.

♦ For a start, when you go out to have a look around, you won't be wearing a backpack.

♦ **Furthermore, you will quickly learn how not to stand out in a crowd.**

♦ Therefore if you carry your things in a money belt, in your hand... you will be much less obvious than walking around with a huge stuffed 'bum bag' strapped to your lower regions!

Yes, there are thieves out there; it's a bad world. However, if you read your local paper, you will see that there are thieves on your doorstep. Have they affected you in a bad way?

Carrying money TOP TIP

1. If you use a pocket, try and make sure that it has a button or a zip. No worries if it doesn't!

2. Back pockets = easy to pick, so get out of the habit if you do it.

3. Make sure that you air out your money belt/neck wallet every once in a while, as if it does get hot/sticky the contents can get a bit damp, and then everything will start to stink!

4. Avoid carrying all your money/credit cards in the same place. Split them up. Some in your day bag, some in your backpack, etc. This will minimise the risk of losing the whole lot.

5. Your day bag should be your most secure possession – your 'mobile safe' as it were. Always keeping it safe, or to hand will ensure that you encounter no problems. At times when it is too bulky to carry around, take with you only the money belt (or whatever you choose to use) and don't let it out of your sight.

6. Good sense and awareness are not for sale in the shops!

The world of bad advice!

I feel that the worst problem here is that maybe too many people are talking to you at the moment about foreigners robbing you blind as soon as you step off the plane in a foreign country. It happened to me, and it'll happen to you. Even yesterday, while I was busking in Plymouth, a woman started talking to me about didgeridoos and Australia... advice for her son. I mentioned about this book, *and she started telling me about all the dangerous places on earth, and where she thought that her son should go*. I asked her where she had actually been abroad. Answer: holidays in Europe! So why is she telling her son where he should or shouldn't go? Because like most of us we are scared, scared of everything unknown. She refused to believe me about how easy it is to travel in Australia for example. I mean, why should I know... I've only done it!

Being safe

The point therefore is… if you are seriously worried about being safe, and carrying your things/money safely… DON'T! If you are reading this part of the book waiting for me to give you a foolproof way of never being robbed of your money, then I'm sorry. I can't/won't do that. Your easiest form of protection for you and your valuables is simply **being aware**. As I said before, you are more likely to be robbed of your valuables in your home town than Kuala Lumpur. However there is a whole section on safety in the book, so have a read to hear some more thoughts on the subject. **My best advice, if you are really worried about it is to stop listening to shitty advice from people who don't know what they are talking about.** They may think that they are helping you, but in the end they are just frightening you. You will be fine.

CHAPTER 11

Hitch-Hiking

"I travel not to go anywhere, but to go. I travel for travel's sake. The great affair is to move." R.L.Stevenson (1879)

This is a unique subject on its own that is dying to have a whole book written about it. I would love to do it as it is something that is very close to my heart; however after writing this book I don't think I'll lift a pen ever again! 30 years ago, so I've been told many a time, everyone would hitch-hike around. Young and old alike, picked up by 'ladies and gentlemen', and dropped off safely with a big smile, a hearty farewell, a piece of apple pie, and with thank you's all round. Those were the days, eh? Unfortunately society changes, a few 'sicko's' appear, and then hitching becomes a dirty word. "You'll never be picked up!" "You'll never get there!" "You'll wait for hours you know!" And these comments are all from people who have hitched thousands of miles in their lives... erm, oh... sorry... *you mean to say that they've never hitched in their life, and that they've never picked up a hitchhiker!* So that obviously gives them the authority to comment on hitch-hiking then! Stories, stories, stories. I've just got one word for it all... **BULL!**

I've hitched in Australia, all the way across Canada (alone), in France, and around the UK. Other friends of mine have hitched around Europe, all over Africa... **and all in the past few years**. "Those were the days?" I'm sorry but, if you approach it correctly, *these are the days*. "They're all long haired wierdos with beards." I have short hair, and always hitch clean shaven. "They're all homeless". Give me a break! "If I pick one up he'll kill me and rape my dog, or vice-versa. They're all dangerous, every one of them!" OK I'll be honest with you, I did squash a spider in the bath a few years back... but that was only because it was asking for it as it refused to move when I asked it nicely! I think you get the message now. We live in a society where everyone is scared... to walk the streets, to be alone, to have doors unlocked. Hey, if you think we're bad, you should go to America!

Let's be serious for a moment.

There is of course the serious issue which I must address. **Unfortunately with the way things are, and the way they will be in the future, society has stopped female hitch-hiking**. Many still do of course, but I think that this is just inviting trouble. Please don't call me sexist when I say that **women shouldn't hitch unless with a companion**. I'm sorry but I've heard a lot of first hand accounts of bad situations, and it just seems that you would be taking too big a risk. Yes, it's true that I've heard a few bad accounts from men, but they sound a lot less frightening. You should also remember that there are other people involved here, i.e. your family. For them to know that you are hitching will be worry enough... but hitching alone! Well, I needn't say any more. You know your parents better than anyone else, so you'll know to what degree they won't sleep, and how much they'll worry.

Please, don't do it.

Why hitch-hike?

For a start it's cheap/free travel. If you do it right then you can normally travel to places just as quick, or even quicker than by bus or train. Quicker than by a plane... you're lying! When you have a series of long journeys to make, chatting to someone really does make the journey go a lot quicker. So why not talk to the person sitting next to you on the plane/train/bus? However, old grannies... beware, use only in desperation, but be ready for photos, irrelevant stories, and some totally remarkable connection to be made between the two of you (like her niece's friend living 4 doors away from your Auntie's chiropodist)... usually leads to the comment "... Tsk tsk... small world, eh?" At this point bail out and head for the toilets, only reappear if she's gone/fallen asleep/passed away!

But the main thing for me is that you tend to meet some very interesting people, and some real characters. As I've mentioned before, most of what I call my 'real education' has come from lifts with a wide variety of people. How else can you really meet the people of a country and get to understand what they are really like. After Canada for example I became really clued up on all aspects of Canadian life. It is only when you learn to appreciate other countries and their people, that you really learn to appreciate your own.

I met people who were extremely happy with their lives, and others who hated their existence. **The thread seemed fairly similar all the way through... you've got to do what you enjoy in life, and do what you really want to do**. From what I witnessed this seemed to be the difference between success and just mere 'existence'. But this is just my point of view, what I saw, and the beliefs which spur me on.

My theory was that if I could hitch across Canada I could do just about anything that I wanted in life, which included getting a good degree, writing this book, and getting a good job. Number 3 hasn't been achieved yet, but I hope that it soon will be.

So you think that you might like to hitch?

If you feel that you're the type of person who fancies the idea, or may even be in a situation where hitching seems the sensible solution, read on. Below I've given you a few rules which I always stick to, and they are proven in that they do work. However, as with a lot of things with this book... guide only please! Find your best method of hitching, stick to it, and you'll get better and better. **If you've never done it before, start off with a very easy distance and see how you get on**. Don't wait to be stuck out in the middle of nowhere with no confidence in yourself. Your body will tend to ooze confidence if it is there, making you as sharp as an infantryman's bayonet. If this gets picked up from 200 metres by a businessman in an Audi doing 80mph... you're on the right track! Depending on circumstances, if I don't get picked up in about 10 minutes, I normally ask myself... why not Tom? If you follow the basic rules and 'play the game' fairly, you should have no problems.

1. **Be confident**, assertive, sure of yourself... look sharp, not spaced out.

2. **Have a sign** and hold it out where it can be seen. It should say where you are going in big bold letters, and should always have a 'Please' in the native language on the bottom... remember you are politely asking for a lift, they have no need to give you one. For sign material you can't beat the side of a cardboard box.

3. Have your **backpack openly visible**. Advertise 'I am a backpacker.'

4. Look **clean shaven and tidy**. In hot countries only wear shorts, T-shirt, shoes and socks (if worn). This shows that you are hiding nothing, and that you really are as harmless as you look.

5. Have a **sign of where you are going next**, or your old sign of where you've been, next to your backpack or somewhere visible. This shows that you are not going to move in with them when you get to the destination, and that you are intending to move on somewhere else.

6. **Stand up straight**, don't crouch, as this is often perceived as a sign that you are hiding something. Smile, laugh, wave, make a show – *enjoy it!* Would you pick up someone looking miserable? No! The last thing you'd want is to

113

try and cheer a hitch-hiker up. Someone else will pick them up. Game over, you lose!

7. **Stand in a place where people are going slow and can stop**. The only way you'll stop a car doing 80 mph is with a rocket launcher! Anyone doing 60 mph+ will see you, and then by the time they've decided to give you ride, will be half a mile down the road, and unable to stop. Oh well, someone else will pick them up... not at that speed! You'll find that people are very selfish and won't skid or crash their cars just to pick you up! **The on ramps to motorways, at traffic lights (the last traffic lights out of town being the best), or just past a roundabout are always the best places**.

A good tip is always to ask locals about where they think the best hitching spot is for you. If necessary get a bus there. Quite often locals are happy to take you the couple a miles there to help you out. It shows you the true kindness of strangers, and anyway, it beats walking there!

The position has got to be right. If there are traffic cones in the way, move them so people can pull over in safety. If they can't pull over they won't. In September 1995 I had to drive 2 miles back on myself to pick up two students from a roundabout in Sheffield. They had been waiting for ages... because they couldn't be seen until you were right next to them, and with the cones it was extremely hazardous to pick them up. I only went back because I thought that they'd never be picked up (and because I'd just come back from Canada and wanted to do a good turn for them, like others had done to me). Point proved I hope.

8. **Be nice**. Many have decided at the last minute to pick me up after I have waved, smiled and said "OK, no problem, thanks!" If you say "Well **** off then!" or have this written backwards on the back of your sign so that it can be read in the rear view mirror, you'll do yourself no favours, and give hitchers a bad name.

9. **Take a flag**. A British flag for example works wonders in Australia, Canada, America, and in a lot of parts of Europe, as well as other English speaking countries of the world. They know that you're a 'real McCoy' backpacker, where you're from, and what language you speak. A lot of people are worried about having an awkward conversation/time with a person with a foreign language. Advertising really helps. If you are miles from home, present yourself properly, and show your nationality, Ex-pats and British tourists will always pick you up. A good lift is a good lift in the end of the day!

10. **Have enough food and drink with you**, emphasis on liquids in hot countries. Also nice to offer to the driver, so they know they won't have to buy you food at any stops.

11. **Engage in interesting conversation**. This is a skill which you will learn

that will always be useful to you. You don't need to be a chatterbox like me, just able to hold a conversation. The driver will then be more willing to take you where you want to go, and less willing to get rid of you at the first opportunity.

12. Carrying on from 11, **becoming 'friends' with the driver** always has the benefit of bonuses such as being offered food and a bed for the night. You may find work, have the chance to stay in a small community for a bit, anything like that. I have been invited to weddings, for Christmas, and always to 'visit again'. They are also welcome over here. It's amazing who you become friendly with!

13. **Check out the car as you approach it**. I turned down a lift in Canada because the driver said that he was going exactly where I wanted to go (a 10 hour drive) to visit his mum. But there was nothing, absolutely nothing, in the car... not even food and drink. Dodgy? Well, I thought so, so I turned him down. He was probably on the level, but I didn't want to take the chance. Children's toys/seats, or for that matter children, are usually a good sign of safety in a car. Businessmen tend to have suits, briefcases and work on the seats. General day-to-day items are also good signs. You'll figure it out. However, only give the car a quick subtle scan, if not they'll think that you're 'casing the vehicle'... and no lift buddy!

14. **Turn down lifts, don't be afraid to do it,** there will always be other ones (of course this doesn't apply to all situations!). If you don't like the situation, turn it down. If they're really OK they'll probably reassure you in some way. If they smell of alcohol... beware! Accidents do happen, more likely if the driver is pissed than not. And of course the simple Golden Rule, **if you're going a long way, try not to take short rides**. It really won't help you if you hop along the motorway from junction to junction.

   This is why it is vital to write the best sign possible. Is the place too far to warrant putting it on the sign? Should you write two or three signs up and aim to get there in stages. Quite often it is useful to hold up the sign of where you want to go finally e.g.. Dover, on the bottom, and somewhere in between on top... London. Even better put on motorways like M1, M25, RN1, on top, so people can see your route... more chance of a longer ride.

15. **Be prepared to give up and take a bus in remote areas** or if it gets late. Without a tent the edge of the road is a nasty place to sleep at night. Even with a tent you are still vulnerable.

16. **Start as early as possible,** because everyone else does if they are going on long journeys. However work out your times... is it rush hour traffic i.e. are they going to work and no further?

17. **Plan your routes carefully,** foodstops, sleeping arrangements, etc.

18. **Would I pick me up?** If answer is "No", sort it out.

19. When you get a ride do **ask the person why they picked you up**. Don't ask this in any kind of menacing way or you're likely to get dropped off asap. But if asked nicely hopefully you'll get a lot of the reasons 1-18, as this is solely what I have based my 'rules' on in the past.

20. When leaving the car, **leave the passenger door open** – to be closed last. Therefore if the person is a bit dodgy or simply forgets that your bag is in the back, they can't drive off leaving you with nothing.

There has always got to be a few 'Don'ts' lying around, right? OK, well here they are:

DON'T

1. **Wear a hat or sun-glasses,** as people like to be able to see your eyes and your face. This can be a bit of a problem in hot, sunny countries if you need shade for your head, so adapt to suit your own needs. Personally I will never wear either of these while hitching, as it is one of the main negatives people who have picked me up tell me about.

2. **Just stick your thumb out.** Genuine people will think... who is he, where is he going? They don't know. You'll wait a while if you try this one. Good luck to you!

3. **Go over the top trying to get a lift.** There is a difference between being funny and looking like an escapee from a nut house. You may also attract nutters.

116

4. **Stand for too long in direct sunlight** as you might well catch sunstroke. This has happened to me twice (something about not learning from your mistakes!). It is not very pleasant, and tends to ruin your day. This stems from me not wearing a hat. So do you or don't you? I can never really decide!

5. **Try and hitch through major cities.** They're very big, and unless your ride is going right through, you won't make it. A tip is to get out on the outskirts and take a bus in and out. If you want to by-pass the city make sure you use the ring roads and get a ride that takes you all the way round. Cities? Avoid them like the plague/talkative old grannies.

6. **Hitch in dangerous places.** I know, seems obvious, but many tend to say "Well it's only a short distance, so I'll risk it." Fools... don't risk it!

7. **Hitch at night**, you're just asking for trouble.

8. **Get dropped off in the middle of nowhere**. Make sure that when you get in the vehicle you establish where they are going first. This will put the driver at ease as he/she will know that you really are safe, and that you are going somewhere. If you end up in the middle of nowhere, you'll find it very difficult to get picked up. People will naturally think that you've been thrown out of a car for some reason.

9. **Take offence**. There is always the odd comedian who will stop, wait for you to get close, and then drive off. Many of you may even have done it in the past. Well, having stitched your sides back up again, and dusted yourself off from where you have been rolling about on the ground in absolute hysterics, carry on hitching. If they were meant to be comedians they would have got jobs on the stage. This has never happened to me, but I have had the thumbs up from all members in the car, jokes and the odd comment. Unfortunately you laugh at them because
a) they're unoriginal
b) you can't hear a word because they've shouted out at 70 mph
c) you're never going to see them again in your life, so are you really bothered anyway!

My overall view on the subject.

You have a maximum of 8 seconds to persuade a stranger that you are harmless enough, and so worth taking in their car. According to the rules above, by the time they pull over they will know that you are:

◆ A harmless backpacker
◆ English, and speak English
◆ Know where you have been

- ◆ Know where you are heading for
- ◆ Hiding nothing
- ◆ Friendly/funny person
- ◆ Clean
- ◆ Polite

☞ *By having a rough idea of the Do's and Don'ts you should have no problems*

As soon as you hear people saying, "Well it's funny, because I've never picked up a hitch-hiker before!" then you know that you're on the right track. "What goes around comes around!" I guess you probably knew that this expression was going to jump out again in this section, so I don't want to disappoint you! Most people who pick you up will have hitched themselves at some point in time. They will tend to look after you, feed you, give you a room for the night, and then take you to a good hitching spot in the morning. Why? Simply because somewhere down the line someone has done it for them, and in the future you will do it for someone else. It's true, I've already helped out a few young people hitching in the UK, something that I will always do, and in turn they will do the same for others.

For me this is the best thing about it. If you can't afford to travel on your own money, you can travel on the kindness of strangers. There is a daft expression which says that, "A stranger is just a friend that you haven't met." Daft, but true? You will have a great time, and get up to all sorts of Shenanigans... like when I was completely led astray by a couple of 'mature' Canadian women, Nina and Tania, in the Rockies. I had a fantastic time, and now have two very good friends.

It can blow your mind!

Be warned, as it can be quite difficult at times i.e. with conversation. People on long journeys will pick you up for conversation to make the time go quicker. Yes time does fly, especially if like me you are naturally chatty and have a lot to talk about. The problem however is when you do a number of hitches a day, which can be a bit of a head spin with the constant repetition of your life story, travels, etc. The conversations will always take the same course, and you'll find that you'll be able to repeat them over and over in your sleep. A good tip therefore is to have something major in the news to talk about. It will also be an education to find out what the average Frenchman thinks about Nuclear testing, Australians about the British Monarchy, and Americans about anything not American (providing you explain it to them first!). Then go on the offensive and ask them questions about their life. No worries, eh?

couple of words about trucks

If you can get rides in them then you are lucky, as they are spacious and comfortable on long journeys, but slow. However you can have a laugh at all the truck stops talking to all the truckers, and hearing what they have to say about life. Great greasy food as well. Diet, what diet! **Unfortunately in a lot of countries it is now becoming illegal for them to pick up hitch-hikers**, mainly for insurance purposes. Therefore they really won't as it means that they will lose their licences. So don't bank on getting their support. However (at the time of writing) it is still possible in the UK.

Where it is legal it is always worth a quick trip to any depots to see if there are any trucks going your way, and to see if one will give you a ride. Beware also if holding a big sign on the side of the road and a big truck roars past. The slip-stream that goes with it can knock you over, and also pull you into the inside lane… so when they go by… hold on to your pants!

Isn't it illegal to hitch in some countries?

Well, so I'm lead to believe. However I personally have had no problems. Generally the police will assess you, and if they feel that you, or anyone else, are not at risk, then they'll turn a blind eye. But from what I have heard from a number of friends is that any women caught hitching will be escorted back to the nearest town, or put on a bus. You see, **it's not me being sexist, it's the law** in many countries. Personally I think that it is a big shame, but then if I had a daughter, I'm sure I would think a whole lot differently.

Is this for you?

Many would like to try it, but are not sure/confident enough to do so. If you are in this category, then why not try hitching a few small distances on an 'A road' nearby which goes from one town to another. For those of you familiar with the Essex/Suffolk border, many a time I have hitched from Stratford St.Mary to Ipswich up the A12, or from Ipswich to Colchester on the A12, and then across to Mersea Island where my parents live. If you find it easy and enjoyable, then go for it. If not… well then you won't bother anyway! Hitching is very easy if done properly, and is very cheap. Like all things in life, practice makes perfect, and by the time you've done it a few times, you'll be a veritable master!

GOOD LUCK!

CHAPTER 12

Tips, Hints and Problems

" 'Old World Charm' means 'No Bathroom'!" LLL

Adapters. Can be bought fairly cheaply. Get a multi-purpose world-wide one. They don't take up much space, and if you do find yourself carrying anything electrical, then you will be able to power it virtually anywhere. **But**, do you really need a hairdryer, iron, electric razor, or a portable beach BarBQ set?

Addresses. You are going to meet, and make, some great friends. Not only that, you are going to meet a lot of them. Naturally you will take a decent address book. The only problem is that a few years down the line Mike Parkinson who used to live in Sudbury UK, will mean absolutely nothing to you, unless you have a very good memory or you keep in contact regularly. A good tip therefore is to note down where you are at the time, and certain characteristics. Mike, for example (who I haven't properly been in touch with since we were in Thailand 3 years ago... this will change, as I am going to make more of an effort!) looked uncannily like Russ Abbot. We happened to pick up on this wee fact... much to his disgust, and so 'Russ' was born. Hence 'Russ' is the name by which I remember who he is. This does seem a fairly obvious thing to do, but if you forget, and end up going to a country and decide to look up an address you have... bummer if you can't remember who it is eh! All I have to say on the subject is Sweden! Addresses are vital to get and keep hold of, especially of people that you got on well with, as the reunion parties and the odd 'long lost friend' kipping on your sofa 'on the way through the UK' is one of the bonuses of travel. It's great having friends dotted all over the world, and very useful too. Once you've got a few you'll feel like a real seasoned traveller, and dead popular too with Christmas cards from all over the world.

Address cards. Carrying on from what I've just written above, a nice idea is to get some personalised name cards printed up, something which can be done virtually anywhere now. If there are a couple of you travelling together there is a great opportunity to get some humorous ones printed, guarantees that people don't forget you! They are also handy to put in the bottom of your bags, so that if your backpack does have the misfortune of getting lost by an airline or by other means, they will know your address and be able to get it back to you asap.

Airport taxes. Check for them at any time when you might be liable to have to pay them. Everyone always gets caught out by them. At the very end of your stay in a country, none of the local currency left... never mind, cos you're getting on a plane to another country, so you'll be all right... get a bit of food on the plane, bit of sleep, time to... DOH! Airport Tax £20 payable before departure thank you very much we accept all major credit cards have a nice day! The hostels will normally be able to tell you how much it is, if there is one at all. However, get in the habit of quickly asking at the airport when you arrive. Saves a lot of hassle!

Backpacks. As have hinted elsewhere in the book, leave home with it as light as possible. Always practise packing, wearing and carrying it before you leave home, so you don't have to undergo major teething problems with it on your first days out whilst you are still trying to find your feet in a new country. You will get used to lumping it around very quickly, and find your techniques quick to master. Your backpack is your house/your secure item. Treat it with respect. If not it will get pissed off with you, deliberately fall apart, and so piss you off. Get a good one... worth paying the money if you have to... and make sure you use the discount at Millets.

☞ *NB Never allow pack to be searched by anyone you would come under the catagory of 'dodgy' in the dictionary, whether an official or not. It is too easy for them to slip something in and then start accusing you. Then the shit will hit the fan. All you have to do (as is your right) is keep hold of the bag and start unpacking it yourself. Don't make a big drama out of doing this, just calmly get on and do it... or you are likely to get nicked.*

Bargaining. Look confident, have cash ready. The first price (in many less developed countries) will be about 3 times the value of the goods, so you know roughly where you are going. But then you will have already have sussed out how much you are willing to pay for the item. The main thing is enjoy it! It's all part of the travelling experience... and if you come away with what you consider to be a bargain, all the better. Don't be offended by any extraordinarily high prices, just realise that in many less developed countries it is good business for salesmen to try and get the best price they can, and if they see a gullible tourist, they will see if they can charge the earth for their goods. What may seem like not too much for us, may seem like a fortune to them. They will get to know pretty quickly that you aren't gullible, and will be quite happy to bargain a proper price. If not, then there is always another shop around the corner. Yes they may well chase you down the street trying to get a sale… and if they do, keep bargaining!

However you must realise the difference between bargaining and just plain 'taking the piss'! If you are offered a handmade waistcoat for £10, and then you turn round and offer 10p, whilst accompanying the offer with a smug grin all over your face… they may well take offence. Don't be rude, be fair. Don't haggle over a matter of a few pence to you, as it really is bad manners! If you are in control, have the cash ready, and treat it all like a bit of fun, you'll do well, and become a bit of an expert within hours. Be serious and ready to walk away at a minute's notice, and you'll find you'll come back home with some real beauties. The only problem is that if your first stops are in these developing countries, and you end up buying a few bits and pieces, they are very bulky, and so a real pain to carry around with you for the rest of your trip. You could think about sending them home (*see* Shipping Items), but this can be risky. What can I say? Common sense I suppose. If it could break, and you've still got a long way to go… should you risk it? As for the bargaining… have fun!

Beaches. Great places to have a lot of fun at, but also a great place to break your neck. Sorry, but I'm not actually kidding on this one. I know of 3 blokes, all my age, who have run into the water and dived in, only to find that there is a sand bank there. It really isn't very nice, so be careful.

Other dangers are swimming in large surf if not used to it, and learning to surf for the first time. If, for the former, you are caught under big waves crashing down on you: don't panic, swim down deep, and let your body go limp every time the wave gets to you. Relax and let the wave take you. And then every time you see a break in the waves, go like ****! for the shore. Learning to surf? Surfboards knock out English people… it is a proven fact! Until you get to the point where you can actually stand on it, make sure you have some sort of spectator there who can pull you out before you drown!

If when learning to surf you find a nice secluded beach with lovely little waves, and then get interrupted by local Aussies who keep shouting 'My Wave' at you… tell them to 'Piss Off'!

Cars. If you've ever bought a car in this country then you'll know what a risk it is. Just imagine the risks abroad then, in a foreign country where it is obvious that you are a tourist, and where you are unlikely to be covered by any major insurances, or helped by any local knowledge. Yet again, a lot of 'fors' and 'againsts' for this one. I know of many people who have found peaches... soft to touch, nice to look at, and sweet... a good deal. But on the other side of the bridge there are the lemons... hard and unpleasant, as they leave a bitter taste in your mouth. In this lottery, unless you know a lot about cars, it really will be down to luck and judgement. Cars bought in hostels can be good, as even though they have been around the clock ten times, and have more spare parts than the Halford's Christmas collection, you know that it does actually run, and that it will get you across America if you pray hard enough. The backpackers that are selling it, although anxious to get a sale, will at least tell you of what they have replaced, and how much they have had to spend on it. They will also tell you all you need to know about how much it will cost you in petrol, insurance, tax, etc. However, once you've taken it for a spin round the block they won't tell you that a) if you go over 55mph that it blows up. b) that if there are more than 2 fairly lightweight people in it then the back tyre will come away. c) that they've been trying to sell it for five months, but everyone apart from you has thought that it is the biggest pile of crap since the 1994 England World Cup campaign, and that they have all gone away in fits of laughter!

TOP TIP!

The other thing to look out for is unscrupulous dodgy looking blokes... you know the sort I'm talking about. Many have been known to advertise their cars on the hostel notice boards, and so are naturally thought to be travellers themselves. These con men will be very good, and will have the most believable stories ready for you. They will check that you are about to drive off miles away, so that when the car does eventually go 'pop!', you'll be so far away that there is nothing you can do about it.

But remember, that if you do buy a second-hand car, there really isn't too much that you can do about it if you have bought a lemon and you know that the bloke who sold it to you knows this. Just make sure that you are insured, and if possible check if any existing cover, e.g. AA, will cover you overseas. I know for example that AA can cover you in America if you have certain policies... so do check.

1. Why not find a local mechanic, slip him a few notes and see if he will have a look at any cars that you are thinking of buying... a few pounds now may

save you a lot of money later on.

2. Ask at the hostel you are staying at... what do they suggest about buying cars in that area/country?

3. If you know that you are going to go to a country with the idea of definitely buying a car and travelling around for a while, why not get to know few of the basics over here first?

4. Embassies have been known sometime to have a few cars... always worth a try.

5. Take time to shop around. Don't expect a Rolls Royce, but don't accept a half loaded skip. You need something reliable. If it looks good, all the better, but your fellow backpackers won't really care.

6. If you buy common makes then you'll always be able to get parts, and they'll probably be cheaper. However, having to wait for specialist parts for your 'Studmobile Mustang peachofacar awsomepower looksfantasticbaby Gti Turbo spoilers wings theworks luckyifikeepitontheground tossers car'... then I'll be the first to laugh at you!

7. When buying, pretend that you are hanging around for a while, get their address so that you can 'call round' if you have any problems. This should help you with the odd 'blagger'.

8. Remember you have to sell it. So allow yourself time, and give yourself a chance by selling it in a major backpacking area, where there is a demand for cars, places like Sydney, New York, etc. Advertise as much as you can, and be prepared to negotiate well. You probably won't regain all the money that you spent, but do try, as the buyers may be very keen to buy and get going. Think about what you wanted to hear when you were buying, and tell it to them. However, if you do have a deadline for when you must leave the country, make sure you do have plenty of time to sell. If not you may end up flogging it off for peanuts, which will really piss you off!

9. Hot countries, old cars may have problems with the air conditioning system packing up. This can affect other parts of the car, and can end up being very costly.

Always pretend like you have an idea about what you are looking at. Learn a few questions to ask. Be confident. You are less likely to be ripped off. Good luck!

Camping. Is definitely cheaper, and can be a really good laugh, depending on the area, time of year, seasons, wildlife, etc. Before going to a big camp site, find out if there will be anyone else there, as there is nothing worse than being the only tent in the middle of a massive national park... unless you like a bit of piece and quiet every once in a while. Check out for local holidays and festivals, as these are the times when the camp sites will be full and lively. In Africa you can virtually stick your tent anywhere. Most developed countries have camp sites with full amenities... yes you can wash, use the

BarBQ's, etc. Many, especially in Australia, will also have swimming pools, as well as many of the hostels offering the opportunity to camp on their grounds for a smaller charge than the rooms. Camping is less secure, but as long as you have some way of securing the tent shut and don't keep your valuables in there, then you should have no problem. Most tents have holes on the zips so you can padlock it shut.

In areas with active wildlife such as bears, **do** heed the warnings such as not leaving food in your tent, eating in your tent, etc. You often hear people saying that after a big night on the beers there is nothing worse than waking up next to someone you don't know. Well there is. Waking up with a hangover to find yourself face to face with a hungry 7 foot Grizzly is a point at which the shit really has hit the fan! It is a fact that in Australia a lot of tourists have been killed by crocodiles whilst posing in ankle deep water next to signs saying 'Beware Crocodiles'. Stupid? Well, I think so. But if you walk around with the attitude that you know it all, and that everything everyone is trying to tell you is irrelevant, then you won't respect nature, and I'm afraid it won't respect you. Camping is cheap, fun, and a great way to meet more of the locals. In these situations you'll find an army of people willing to watch your tent for you, and always invitations for beer, dinner, etc. A great way to meet people and understand their way of life.

Chill Out! Stepping off an aeroplane onto the hot tarmac of an unfamiliar country, an unfamiliar language, and what seems like a multitude of gabbling people, all running around, eyeing you up, etc., can be daunting. This kind of situation can scare the pants off anybody, whether 18, just out of school, and just landed in the first country, or 24, a graduate, and a seasoned traveller. Whether it is Sydney, Delhi, Marrakech or Mexico City, it will always seem overwhelming and possibly too much to handle. The secret is not to walk to the other end of the airport and book yourself on the first plane back home, but... to chill out. Take a deep breath, and remember that you are there to enjoy yourself, and that you have all the time in the world.

The best thing to do is find your way to the hotel/hostel/campsite/etc., dump all your things (ensure they are safe, if unsure, take all the important bits with you) and then go 'walkabout'. Have a wander. For your first wander, relax and have a little look at everything in your surroundings. Avoid looking at maps and guidebooks, as this does tend to advertise yourself as a tourist, and may make you look a bit vulnerable. Just place your things in a normal plastic bag, and wander around without bringing attention to yourself. Take in the surroundings, and you'll soon get used to the sound of the language, the smells, the way of life, etc. If people do come up and talk to you, ask yourself why. Don't get lost, be wary of where you walk, and have the name and address of where you are staying written down on a piece of paper, so that you'll always be able to find your way back.

When you get back, I always find that getting a few beers inside you tends to help. After a few everything seems a lot easier, slower and less overwhelming. A few more on top of that and suddenly everything seems easy, friendly and familiar. Even more, and then (for me) all the women turn into famous supermodels, and they're all in love with me. And then I normally wake up with a stinking hangover. Well there's a little bit more about me that you didn't really need to know... but what the hell!

Credit cards. Always useful to have in emergency situations, as they are an invaluable source of 'large amount of money quick'. They are also handy for their insurance purposes, and very useful for providing emergency aid to distant countries when needed. Remember the Barclaycard advert with Rowan Atkinson with the guy with the leg infection 'You're looking for his Barclaycard Bof? This is no time to go shopping! No... I'm going to have to locate the wound and suck the poison out myself!' In the end the bloke is airlifted out. When I met Amanda Fogg in Indonesia, she told us about her friend who, whilst in India, had some sort of stomach upset, and so 'blocked it up' with Lomotil. This is usually a good idea, however in this case she must have blocked the infection in, and so it festered and got worse. The result was that she was desperately ill, and Amanda feared for her life. In desperation she rang one of the credit card companies on their emergency number. Within 24 hours she had been flown back to a hospital in England. She recovered. A true story, and one which I always use to remember to keep those emergency numbers safe. Because in the end of the day, when push comes to shove, if there is an emergency and you need help, these boys will move mountains.

Beware... as in some of the poorer countries of the world they are very good at making fakes. There have been occasions where numbers have been taken, signatures forged, and extra zeros added. You will only find out about this when you eventually get home, and there really isn't much that you can do about it. So to be sure, make sure that you take the carbon copies (which you are entitled to do), and in cases where you are not sure about the credibility of the shopkeeper, don't hand your card over until you have at least 3 character references, a certificate of reliability from their government, and proof that the bloke does in fact own the shop that you are standing in! If in doubt, try and pay by other means.

Courier flights. At the very time of writing I am actually on one of these courier flights, using it for my own needs, but also as a bit of a 'road test' for this book. This is a fantastically cheap way to travel, but is relatively unknown. How it works is that certain airlines (British Airways for example) have a system where they can make you a courier for the day. When boarding the plane you will be given a set of documents which you will in turn hand to someone to put in the plane's safe. Once you get on to the other side, you pick up the documents and hand them to someone else as soon as you get off the plane. The documents are all business documents, and so fully security checked. You are required to be 18+, and to wear smart clothes. You get the usual baggage allowance, and the ticket is non-refundable. The only drawback is that you have to set a date to return by, and you are normally bound to a maximum of one or two weeks depending on where you go to. However it is extremely cheap, quite often cheaper than a one way ticket if you are going to buy one of those anyway. But be warned, it is a very popular way to travel, as it is so cheap. Flights go every day, and so if you put your name forward early you can just about go whatever day you want to. For more information write to:

BA Travel Shop,
1st Floor,
Export Cargo Terminal,
World Cargo Centre (S126),
Heathrow Airport,
Houndslow,
Middlesex. TW6 2JS
Tel: (0181) 564 7009 Lines will be busy, so just keep trying.

Changing your plans? Make sure you let someone know. By keeping in regular contact with people this will cause no problems. However, if you are expected in one place, but are 'largeing it up' somewhere else, then you may cause others needless anxiety.

Creases in your clothes? Just at the point where you don't have an iron and you are out to impress? Well, no more! Simply get hold of a few pairs of old tights. Then pull the item of clothing up into the tights. You will be left with a big sausage shaped thing that you can simply coil into your bag. When you take the garment out... hey presto, no creases!

Cultural-practices. Make as much effort as possible to learn and respect them. In parts of the world the right hand is for eating, the left is for the toilet, and gifts should be given and accepted with two hands. If you are left handed, think about this for a while, as it is often the ultimate insult to pick things up with the left hand, even though you have been doing it for years.

Dehydration. Very easy to get dehydrated, but easily avoided by constant drinking. Ensure when buying bottled water that there is a good seal on the bottle, and that it hasn't been tampered with. You can make a lot of money by filling old bottles up with bad water, and then selling it as the good stuff!

However if you do get dehydrated, just drink plenty of water mixed with salt and sugar. Then take a rest. You should be restored in no time. If you find yourself getting dehydrated on a regular basis, you may find that you have some diabetic tendencies. This does not mean that you are a diabetic (unless you are of course!), but you should be aware that you might well be prone to headaches, dizziness, etc. if you don't get enough liquid.

Didgeridoo. A classic Australian instrument whose sweet rhythmic sounds are played by me on the streets of the UK for the entertainment of the public!

Diet. No I'm not talking about 'fatty busters' for all you women out there who are obsessed by your weight, and who give us blokes hell if we even bring the subject up, and of course hell when we avoid the subject. So we're in a no win situation. But can we tell you that… lads, are you with me on this one! Anyway, I'm digressing again. Watching your diet is the point of this little Tiperoony. It is very easy to live off fast food when you are travelling… burgers, chips, hot dogs. In a few of the Asian countries it is easy/safe to go with what you know best… Pizza! All very well, but when you are travelling it really is essential to think about what you eat, and to make sure that your body does get what it needs.

Fruit is good for you and cheap. This is from someone who never used to eat any fruit. I now make sure that I do eat an orange or an apple a day. However, when buying fruit off the street, don't eat it straight away, take the skin off, and make sure that the skin is not pierced. Oranges therefore are safe, as well as giving you a good balance of Vitamin C. Granola bars/muesli bars. Again you are looking at someone who looked at these on the shelf and then picked up the Mars bar next to it. Believe it or not they don't actually taste like they look – sawdust! – but are actually very tasty. These chewy/crunchy fruit and oat bars are good for you, and will give you energy that is much needed when walking around a lot. Bananas are again very good for you, and are often a lot tastier and bigger than the ones that you get over here. Porridge/oats are again cheap and good for you. The sachets are easy to store, there are lots of different flavours, and all you have to do is add water. It is one of those foods that 'sticks to your ribs' in the morning, and sets you up for the day.

Do bear in mind that I am not someone who eats like a sparrow. In fact I do eat like the proverbial 'pig'… I'm not shy when it comes to food! If you are like me, you might find it a bit of a hassle/expense to fill those hollow legs. However rice, pasta and bread are the easy options. Carbohydrate city! If you have an appetite like that then you'll probably burn it all off anyway. The only thing is that you may have to learn a few little culinary skills, simple enough to make that pile of rice/pasta taste anything but dull. This is not only for those greedy buggers like myself (but just to depress you... I can eat as much as I like, but still only stay a slim, and well proportioned, 10 stone... sorry!)

If you can't cook, it's about time that you did learn a few of the basics now. You'll find that if you are staying at a particular hostel for a week or so, and if they do have kitchens with fridges, cookers, cutlery, etc. (as most do), then it is cheaper to do a shop at the beginning of the week which will last you for the week. You can then get into the habit of cooking yourself a good decent meal everyday. This will be a lot cheaper than buying each day. This also turns out a lot cheaper if you are travelling with others and you agree to share the cost of the food. Cooking and eating together will then take away the pain of being in a kitchen, if it is as appealing to you as swallowing the contents of Bernard Manning's dirty underwear drawer!

Drugs. If it is in your nature to delve a little in these murky waters, make sure you take the highest precaution. In most of the countries that you go to drugs will be a lot cheaper than you are used to, and in much more abundant and open supply. Being a traveller in some places will mean that you will be offered them left, right and centre. This is what your parents fear, and in certain places, they are right. However if you are not into them, it is easy to say no and be left alone. Despite what your parents or other 'wise' people have told you, you will not be chased or harassed until you buy some. These people know that there will probably be someone who will buy round the corner, and anyway they won't want to draw attention to themselves. If you do intend to buy, take the following advice:

♦ In some countries there is still the death penalty for being involved with drugs.

♦ You really don't know what you are getting. The drug may be different to what you normally get at home. This could be lethal to you, or do you untold damage.

♦ It is not unknown for corrupt officials, or bloody good con men, to sell you something and then threaten to have you arrested. If you are young, out in Africa/Asia/South America, and now face the possibility of a long jail sentence, or possibly even the death penalty, you will pay anything they ask for. In this position you will be blackmailed/robbed of hundreds of pounds.

♦ In situations such as #3, don't try and fight it. You have been caught out, and you will have to learn by it and pay financially for the consequences. If they are corrupt enough to actively go out to get you, they will be corrupt enough to see that you suffer if you don't play by their rules. Always pay the price, and get out ASAP. And then, most importantly, learn by it.

♦ Heard stories of drugs being dropped in drinks?... if it happens here in the UK, why not on the other side of the world? I've never heard of it happening, but to prevent it, get in the habit of holding/carrying your drink with your hand over it. If you put up some form of protection, it won't be tried.. they will only try anything like this if it is easy and guaranteed to work.

♦ Drug smuggling. Well if you try this then you're a bigger pillock than I think you realise. I suggest you have a sit down and have a really good think about your life.

There have been cases of drugs being put into unsuspecting people's bags so that it can be smuggled across the border. Very rare, and easily avoided by keeping a very good eye on all your belongings all the time. You will invariably be with others on a border crossing, and so you are unlikely to be chosen as they have to somehow get the drugs back on the other side. You are no good because they won't be able to get to you or the bag without being seen. Very unlikely then.

☛ **NB: All of the above are either very unlikely, or can easily be avoided by your own actions.** I am not trying to fuel the paranoia of worried parents, or your own fears generated by various programmes or articles that you may have read. I am a great believer in the idea that if you are aware of these things, then you will be able to face up to them and deal with them. It will also be no shock to you if you go to a place like Bali, and in the middle of the street an Indonesian will slide up to you and whisper 'Mushrrrrooms... mushrrrrrooms... you want to flyyyy to the moon tonight... !'. 'Eeeeerm... nno thank you very mmuch, we're just off down to the beach... But I'm sure the moon's very nice this time of year... see ya!' as you hurry away. No problem, dealt with.

So please don't worry, just be aware. I've been offered drugs in Manchester and even lowly old Ipswich on the streets. It happens, it's a part of life. Just as long as you know to watch your luggage at border crossings, and after you have packed to leave the country. Also to be suspicious of anyone taking an unnecessary interest in your flight details, home address, etc. before you leave. If you do buy from someone on the street, check that what you have is what you paid for, and that the person selling it isn't an undercover police officer, or a con man who when offering you 'grass', really does mean... grass! Just be cool about it all, eh?

Eggs. How do you know if they are OK to eat? Why... roll them of course! If they are a bit dodgy they will roll OK. If they are good to eat, then they will not roll properly and wobble all over the place (as the yolk moves around). Also bad eggs float in water; good eggs sink.

Embassies. Can't bail you out, but will always be there to advise you and get you any help that you need. Any problems, don't be afraid to go to the

Embassy, or to get in touch with them. (*See* 'Health and Emergencies' and the numbers in the back of the book.)

Expensive Hotels. Have good toilet facilities if the ones that you are exposed to just will not do. A special mention must go to Raffles Hotel in Singapore, which in my opinion has a 5 star set of dunnies, and for the lads, self flushing urinals as soon as you take a step back. What else could a man (or woman) want?

First Aid course. These can be done through the St. John's Ambulance. If you have time, try and take one before you go. It is very useful to have, and could save you a lot of pain, time and worry if you know how to look after/treat yourself properly. You may well end up saving someone else's life someday too.

Flights. I used to enjoy flying, but after a string of flights, the novelty soon wore off, and the whole shebang of airports, planes, flying lost its appeal.

Tips are:

◆ Ask for it! If you prefer a window or aisle seat, ask for it. Similarly with smoking, non smoking, and vegetarian meals.

◆ On long flights, always find out if it is a full flight. If empty, see if you can get one of the middle seats so that you have plenty of room, and so be able to stretch out over the 4 seats when you want to sleep. In those situations all you are going to see from the window are the clouds and, anyway, when you land you can probably jump into a free window seat to see the view as you come in.

◆ If you like to watch the films, ensure that your seat is not too close/too far away from the screen. Ask at check in. Be nice. This can make/break a flight.

◆ As you are booking in advance always check the arrival time of when you land, as the last thing that you need is to fly in to somewhere in the middle of the night with no accommodation, and no knowledge of where to go.

◆ Big flights always have food wastage of some kind. If you are hungry, being nice and polite to the stewards/esses normally brings you the benefit of a 2nd or even a 3rd meal (a 4th one time... good old Quantas – well I was fairly hungry at the time!) Backpackers are often seen as easier passengers for the airline staff – rarely complaining, and grateful for what they get. Furthermore they are more relaxed travellers, and so are usually pleasant and interesting to talk to. Getting to know your steward/ess on long flights makes your flight, and their job a lot better. On the flight into Australia we were fed beer after beer, extra portions, the works. It was one of the best flights that I have ever had.

◆ Overbooked flights: two fantastic words that as a backpacker you can take full advantage of. As you have all the time in the world, when you hear that the flight is overbooked, go immediately to the flight operator and offer your seat up. You will become their best friend as it helps them out, but you will also do yourself a massive favour as you will be fully compensated. To give you an idea you may get a night in a 5 star hotel, cash bonuses, meals, free upgrades, etc. I just missed out on one when I came back from Canada, and I was absolutely gutted! If you get one, just don't tell me about it as I'll probably throw up!

◆ If you are pleasant/charming to the check in employee, and ask really nicely, they may well give you and free upgrade into business class. Again I have known this to happen, but despite asking thousands of times, I have got absolutely Jack Shit... and I can be a real charmer when I want to at times (although I'm not admitting that, I'm just using it to illustrate a point!)

◆ Waiting at airports. Again, try and chill out about it. Remember that you have all the time in the world. So the plane is delayed – big deal, who cares... you shouldn't. Just ensure that in your day bag that you have everything that you need to keep yourself occupied. You'll probably find yourself amongst a group of backpackers, and so you'll all join up, start chatting, and then the time will fly anyway. You can also use these moments as an excuse to go up to people (especially if travelling alone) and make a few friends... some may be going to the same place as you at the other end, so you'll discuss plans, share taxis, etc.

Food. Beware as in all countries the food will be prepared in ways that you will not be used to. If you struggle through a meal, drinking copious amounts of water, and then devouring 4 ice creams at the end, and then in the morning whilst on the toilet your arse goes down for a drink... you will realise that it was in fact red chilli, and not tomato, that you were eating!

Gung Ho travellers. These boys (and girls of course) are usually recognised by the crazy nicknames they have, and the bull-shit advice that they give. Yes you may think that Pyscho and Adrenalin 'Junkieman' Dave are a great laugh and have got a lot of stories to tell in the bar... but in the end of the day would you share a room with them without checking their names against those on Interpol's 'Most Wanted' list first? These are the guys that will drink and drive, go where they really shouldn't, and will say they have been where they really haven't. They won't be around when you decide to engage in some of the local customs they have bragged about, or gone surfing in shark infested waters with the knowledge that all it takes is 'one hard smack on the nose and the big woosy shark will run away with tears in its eyes'... it won't!

Guide books. Like this one should be treated as 'guide only'. Yes it may well be the best madras in the world in the restaurant 4 doors away from the

main youth hostel in Kuala Lumpur, but if you find that the restaurant is packed with backpackers all sweating over a madras, and reading the same book... !

Hello! Have you seen all the other empty restaurants down the road with similarly good (and probably cheaper) menus? Probably just as good. Try not to walk around with your head down ticking off all the places in the guide books. You have spent a lot of money to come a long way. By all means use the guide books for reference, but remember to look up and take everything else in as well.

Gifts. It may be illegal to bring them back in to the UK, or to take them out of the country, so do try and find out before you buy a 7 foot python, lug it all the way round Asia, only to find the guy at Heathrow taking it off you... it'll only piss you off!

Hairdressers. Can you cut hair? Do you own some clippers? If so, here's an idea for you. On the 'backpacking circuit' there are always those who put adverts up for haircuts. If you have hair like mine that goes afro (Michael Jackson aged 5 – that's me after 6 weeks without a haircut!), it needs to be cut… this can be expensive. By doing the odd haircut here and there you will:

◆ earn your rent for the night or even longer
◆ keep yourself fed for a week if you do loads
◆ get yourself known and find it easy to make friends
◆ become very popular

Just remember to put a notice up on the hostel notice board wherever you stay, stating where you are, how long you'll be there, and the price. If you keep it cheap, you'll always find plenty of business.

Health. This is very important, and so needs major care and consideration. General travelling around will keep you fit, and will make you fitter with the amount of walking and swimming that you may do. You'll find that it's cheaper to walk to the shops/town and back, and having all the time in the world, good weather, etc., you may find that you'll be walking 4 miles a day and not even noticing. Bus fares are expensive, so I always choose the walking option. Also the time spent outdoors will do wonders for your respiratory system, but watch out for polluted cities like Bangkok where the effects of the heat and the pollution quite literally did my head in. However you're sure to notice the difference a bit of time outside in the good weather does to you.

However it is when you feel that there is possibly something wrong with you that you must watch out for yourself. I'm very guilty of this, thinking that if I ignore it that the symptoms will go away. What if it doesn't and it gets worse…? You are a long way from home and your local GP. There are countless stories of backpackers who think that they have the symptoms say of a cold, but find that it turns in to some local/Southern Hemisphere disease.

◆ I picked up 'Tropical ear' out in Australia, very painful, simply from not drying my ears out properly after swimming.
◆ Cerebral malaria feels like sunstroke… nausea, dizziness, etc.
◆ Giardia (Amoebic dysentery) is a very bad food poisoning that starts with stomach cramps.
◆ Bilharzia, caught from swimming in inland lakes or rivers.

Now this isn't an excuse for all you hypochondriacs out there to start feeling ill at every possible moment thinking that Malaria is setting in. It probably isn't… all I'm saying is that if you really aren't well, get yourself looked at, and treat yourself properly. As mentioned above it is well worth taking a

St John's Ambulance course before you go, just so you do know how to treat yourself and what to look for.

THE SUN can be very dangerous. However wearing a hat avoids sunstroke, and skin cancer is avoided with good high factor suncreams and staying out of the midday sun. Worried about getting a suntan? Well you're going to be away for long enough, so I wouldn't worry about that… just take your time. Be warned, the sun is surprisingly hot! I don't normally burn, and go brown very quickly due to my olive skin… I started off with Factor 6 in Fiji, and burnt like an absolute bugger! Painful – yes. Don't do it… you tan just as well with a 15.

AIDS and STD's are easily avoided by taking precautions and with safe sex. Get in the habit of washing your hands before you eat, and be 'choosy' about what you eat. Eat healthily, but be careful about seafood, water, ice, salad, i.e. what things are washed in, and what you brush your teeth in. These are things that you will quickly learn to look out for, learning by other people's experiences, and by watching what they do/don't do.

It'll grow on you and you'll form good habits. the last thing I want for you is to get paranoid and take all precautions neccessary… your own natural defences will tend to weed out anything that you really shouldn't do/eat anyway. If you go away with the thought of looking after yourself, then you'll be fine. The odd dose of 'traveller's tummy' (or the 'galloping trots' as it was affectionately known by Tony and I) is a pain, but has never really hurt anyone. We all get it sometime, and laugh about it later.

NB Beware of appendicitis: a sharp pain down on your left hand side below your stomach. If it hurts, it needs to come out and soon. The only way is to get it whipped out as soon as possible. If you haven't had your appendix out then you should be aware of the problem, symptoms, and what to do. So do ask your doctor about this one when you go for your check up and jabs.

Insurance. Always have insurance, you'd be daft not to. But the type of insurance obviously depends on what you intend to get up to, and where you intend to go to get up to these things! If you intend right from the start to go bungy jumping, rock climbing, skiing, crocodile wrestling and bare back elephant boxing, then you must make sure that your insurance policy will cover you. A few of them nowadays have that little bit of small print included which may not cover you for some of the above, so make sure you ask at the time of buying your insurance. Read the whole policy and question anything odd.

MEDICAL INSURANCE – don't mess around, just make sure that you are fully covered with it. If you do yourself a bit of damage in any country that isn't your own, it is going to cost you. Furthermore if you do yourself a bit of damage in a country where you don't speak the language, and whose national debt is equivalent to the amount of money you spent on your ticket... you will be stung. Not having full insurance could lead you into hot water, and possibly mean you having to cut short your trip... and for the sake of saving an extra £100 or so before you go, you'd be a pratt not to do it!

♦ **Shop around**. Like everything else, hunt around for the cheapest and best insurance that you can find. Cover yourself for the full duration of the trip, and ask about what you should do (and what it will cost) if you want to extend your trip and the insurance. You can insure yourself with anyone, however:

♦ If you ask the company you are booking your ticket with, they might offer you a good insurance deal included in the ticket.

♦ If you book with a credit card, you might find yourself insured by the credit card company as well. However these are only good for extra cover, as they don't give you full cover on everything that you may need... but do check out what you are entitled to.

♦ Does the insurance cover 'Repatriation'?

♦ **Read the small print,** or get it explained to you by the agent. Just to highlight the above point, to be airlifted of a mountain in Nepal will cost you more than just a fiver and a pair of Levis nowadays. It will cost you thousands. Make sure you are covered for medical expenses, luggage, passport, tickets, etc.

♦ **Baggage insurance.** I don't bother with this any more as I've never lost or had anything stolen. My opinion is that clothes can all be bought again very cheaply. However if you are carrying an expensive camera, walkman, pair of pants, then maybe it would be advisable to you.

♦ **Cancellation insurance.** You may be offered this initially so that if you have to cancel then you won't lose all your money. Again this will all depend on your circumstances and peace of mind.

The main thing about insurance is to assess what you are really going to need and what you think you could do without. On your rounds you will be offered all sorts of insurance which may give you a bit of a headache, so the best thing to do is sit down with somebody and get them to offer you their best insurance, and then take that offer off to the next person and see if they can do better.

However don't skimp on insurance just for the sake of a few bob, as if it ever comes to the time that you will need it, then you'll be wanting all the cover that you can get. Be safe and sure... full medical and all the other trimmings that you will need.

NB If travelling with a companion it may be worthwhile informing them about what type of insurance (particularly medical insurance) you have.

Claiming on your insurance. No matter what the event is, make sure you get hold of all the evidence, receipts, etc. If there has been some type of accident make sure you get photos of anything that you think will help your claim. Remember that the guys who will be assessing your claim will be miles away, and only have your evidence to go on. If there is a police report on the incident, get copies of it. *Get everything you possibly can and the claim will go through quicker and you should have more success.*

Still unsure about insurance?
If you have any questions, or if you think that you're not covered properly, ring **(0171) 600 3333**, and you will get through to the **Association of British Insurers** who will give you advice and full explanations.

Injections. When you go to your Doctor for your check up, make sure that it is done a good few months before you go, so that you have plenty of time for them to stick loads of needles in you. If like me the thought of injections and needles sounds as appealing as having an umbrella opened up in your bottom, don't worry. It doesn't actually hurt that much, the worst will be like a bee sting at the most. Turn away, close your eyes and grit your teeth… or if you think you're hard… ask them if you can do it yourself! **The doctors will be able to tell you which injections you will need, and you do need them, so go and get them done, and then keep photocopied evidence of them.**
NB Try to get a Havarix injection from your GP, as it lasts for 10 years for Hepatitis A. Might as well get it over and done with now, eh?

Jobs/working abroad. Make sure that you have all the necessary visas if you want to work in any of the countries that you are to visit. The most popular is the Working Visa for Australia, which you can get on the spot from the Embassy in London. If deciding to work in Australia, make sure you apply for a 'Tax File Number' as soon as you can, as you'll need it if you get work which is taxed… or don't bother and get taxed at a rate of about 50%… it's up to you! Remember all your photocopies of any educational qualifications that you may have. This visual proof may be the difference between you being given the job or told to ring back in a couple of weeks. A driving licence is sometimes essential to have. You see the thing about backpacker work is that if you really want it, and you look around… you'll find it. Employers are always looking to take backpackers on because quite often there is a bit of work that takes about a week/fortnight to do. So they will be quite happy to take you on because they know that you might only want a couple of weeks work before you move on. Cash in hand, no working visas needed, and you'll be long gone. Perfect!

However do be aware of **backpacker exploitation**. This can happen in 'picking' farms such as the bananas, mangoes, pineapples, etc. It is hard work, it can be an experience, and it can be very well paid. But before you get taken out to the back of beyond and so are at the owner's mercy (as you get taken miles out of town and so are stranded if you don't want the job) find out exactly what you have to do to earn the money, what they might expect you to pay them, and how much money you will realistically be left with at the end of the week. Why? Because many are offered a lot of money to go and pick fruit, and then find out that they are charged a ridiculous amount for food and accommodation, transport, a picking licence, special picking shoes, owner's holiday, daughter's car, etc. However don't be put off by this. If you ask the questions first then the honest farmers will make themselves clear to you… dishonest ones will tell you to clear off as you will probably put gullible backpackers off. With the honest ones, if you put the hard graft in you can earn a lot of money.

Unless desperate try to find work that you enjoy, don't be forced into work you don't like purely for the sake of working. Look around for jobs, and don't be afraid to do a bit of bargaining with the employer… remember that you 'don't actually exist' in Australia (make of that what you will!). If you are confident enough go out and look for work, ask everywhere you go i.e. offer to do work in the hostels in exchange for food and accommodation… in fact in Australia for example many hostels do this anyway. Good luck!

Keeping in touch. *See* the section under 'Parents'.

'Kind people'. May offer you food or drink. Why? Make sure you are aware of their intentions as mugging people whilst under the influence of drugs has been known to happen in some countries; it even happens here in the UK. However the sixth sense that you will develop will allow you to distinguish between these and the genuine offers. Sometimes it is a good idea not to spurn offers as it may well cause offence. In these situations an exchange of gifts is a great idea and may well get you a long way… so those balloons, pens, English postcards I've mentioned under **'Packing'** may be a good idea after all!

Locals. I have mentioned locals throughout the book. Maybe I should label this under 'culture shock', because I feel that this is the main problem that causes the concern and anxiety when faced with 'locals' for the first few times. The main tips are just simply to be aware. If you arrive at an airport or a bus station in a few less developed countries and find yourself surrounded by what may seem like thousands of locals, the main thing to do is not to panic. If you are a bit claustrophobic, you may struggle a bit in the throng of people trying to get your attention. Being a Western backpacker you are seen simply as a Westerner who has money… and compared to the great majority of people that you will meet, you are relatively wealthy. You may be offered everything from taxi rides to watches, from sex to massages.

- Take a deep breath and relax, you are perfectly safe.
- Keep an eye on your belongings as thieves may take advantage of the crowd and your confusion.
- If there are other backpackers around, stick with them… always a good idea to get talking to other backpackers on the planes/bus who are going to the same destination, remembering that you are all in the same boat. You are then less likely to get ripped off, will feel more secure, and will instantly make some friends.
- If you are by yourself, keep all your money hidden, find out exactly where you want to go, and then find some sort of information place and ask how much you should be paying to get to wherever you want to go. Once you feel confident, go outside and start to haggle a price. This is a talent which will literally grow on you.
- **My favourite technique** is to pull one of the locals confidently to the side, haggle what you think is a decent price, and don't give him the money until you get there and are satisfied that you are actually where you are meant to be.
- Practice always makes perfect, and remember that as a traveller it is your duty to be ripped off every once in a while… it happens to everyone (they're lying if they say otherwise!), just don't get offended if you have lost out on the equivalent of about 10p, forget about it.

TOP TIP!

Beware giving locals the money before you actually get the full service that you have paid for. If they turn round at the end and charge you again, you haven't got a leg to stand on. Half now, and half when we get there seems to do the trick. Try not to get too ripped off!

I hope you realise that I am playing on your worst fears here, taking the worst case scenario that you may have in your head from watching films/documentaries, and so throwing you in at the deep end as it were. The truth is that it will never be as bad as you may think. You will invariably be with other backpackers and so find it very easy and safe indeed. However I'm a great believer in that if you expect the worst, everything else from then on in will be easier than expected.

◆ Never give addresses to locals except in very special circumstances. Everyone will be your friend if there is something that they can get out of it. So be warned. I have been hit by this one. I gave my address to a very polite, educated, good natured, wealthy Malaysian girl we met on a train, who was after an English pen pal to practice her English with. The first letter was very nice, talking about her life, hobbies, etc. But what I wasn't ready for was the stream of letters that followed from all of her friends asking for marriage, names and addresses of my friends, photos, etc... not very pleasant!

Languages. Learning key phrases I've found to be a great way of getting what you want. Starting off in their language unless fluent gets you nowhere, as you are left staring at them like a perplexed pike as they gabber on at you in gobbledegook as the only phrase you know translated means 'Good morning sir/madam, and how are you this morning?'... and then they tell you! Bad move. Start the conversation in your broken 'Tourist speaks English to local but with a fake French accent'... to establish the ground rules, and then throw in the odd bit of badly pronounced Thai for 'How much is it?' normally said with my cheeky grin and a little smile. This is

TOP TIP!

Chat up lines in virtually every language under the sun (especially Swedish) can come in very handy, but then that's a different story altogether!

always appreciated, and gets you a long way. Never get the local to write it down for you, always write it in your diary how it sounds to you, e.g. 'Nissan bulla'... which is 'Good morning, how are you?' in Fijian... a very polite thing for you to say to a Fijian, and they love it! Easy to remember... the new 4x4 from Nissan, the Nissan bulla!

Late Arrival. If you book the hotel in advance you can just say 'Hotel Bodeglas, Mr Taxi Driver'. It may be good or bad, but at least it will be a bed for the night and will save you the hassle of faffing around late at night in unfamiliar territory. You can then sort yourself out in the morning.

Litter. If this is a bad habit of yours, please get out of it, and don't do it at places such as Ayers Rock, Taj Mahal, Himalayas, or in my street/house/bedroom. It's a disgusting habit, you're lazy, no more said.

Maps. don't flap about with them in unfamiliar places too much as they point you out to anyone who cares to notice that you are a tourist and that you're probably lost. If you are lost ask reputable people who live in houses or work in reputable companies. If they have one leg, sleep rough in the docks, wear an eye patch, and answer to the name of 'Blackbeard', maybe you want to think about it first.

Mechanics. Are you one? Do you know your way around the engine of a car? Well if you've read the part on 'Buying cars' (page 122) then you may well be thinking of a way to earn some money/make friends. When staying in major backpacker places such as Sydney, Cairns, New York, Toronto, etc. make sure that you advertise your services in all the major hostels as it really is a great way for you to earn a bit of money. If you can confidently assess cars for other backpackers then you will soon find that you are worth your weight in gold on the backpacker circuit. So **GO FOR IT!**

Mopeds/motorbikes/bicycles. Beware when you hire them as there is a scam about where they follow you to your first stopping point, wait for you to leave the bikes unattended, whip them, and then charge you for the price of a bike. Just be aware. Also be very wary of renting them in places like Asia where the roads and the bikes are very badly maintained. Sometimes it can be downright bloody hairy, especially when you find yourself heading downhill doing 60mph on a moped designed to do 30mph tops, with no brakes, but being overtaken by some loony local who's suddenly up for a bit of a race 'weeth thiiis crayzy man from Eeeeengaaaland'! Beware.

Musical instruments. Always great for meeting people/as a talking point. Guitars are always the favourites, and by the time you come back you will have improved considerably. However, whatever you take, don't take the

141

instrument that you've had for years, as you'd be gutted if you lost it… ge
a cheap alternative. As for travelling with them – it is possible, just a bit awk
ward at times. However I carried my didgeridoo halfway round the world
as well as a surfboard for a while when we were in Australia… it's worth it
so you manage!

Nausea. If brought on by say travel sickness can be relieved by ginger (to be
taken orally of course!). If suffering from sea sickness try to keep your eyes
fixed on a cloud as it tends to balance your eyes and make you feel better.

'No Go areas'. Find out where they are, and, well, avoid them… or at least
let the 'gung ho' travellers from page 132 go there first and see how they get
on before you make your decision.

Passport.

◆ Ensure now that it is fully up to date and valid for the whole duration of your trip. Trying to renew it with only a few days to go before your plane takes off will only be a major hassle to you, something which you don't need. As for trying to get it renewed when you are thousands of miles from home and moving from country to country… ever tried picking your nose with a pneumatic drill? I think you get the picture… incidentally, what a thought, eh?

◆ Check your 'dodgy' stamps as there are some countries that you may find it difficult to get into, such as the Arab and Israeli countries, and anywhere in the West if you are an active member of the PLO.

◆ Are you dual nationality? If so, do try and get both passports up to date as it may mean more work opportunities for you, and definitely less queuing time at certain countries' borders.

◆ **Although technically yours, your passport is strictly the property of the British Government.** In the case I outlined above of a few people hiring out mopeds and nicking them back, they usually get away with it by holding your passport as a deposit. Many are simply 'mugged' of their money just to get their passport back. Whereas the answer should be that whenever anyone decides to mess around or play games with you (effectively holding you to ransom with the use of your passport), get in touch with the Embassy straight away, as they don't tend to see the funny side, and will basically get your passport back for you, and maybe bring the issue up with the local police. In this case the mopeds are covered by the insurance anyway. So don't let them piss you around. It is your right to keep hold of your passport and documents at all times.

◆ In a situation where you think that it may be a bad move to let them out of your hands… don't. Just keep hold of them and allow the appropriate people to watch as you turn the pages yourself… however don't do this in a way to antagonise the authorities, as you will only end up wasting your time and maybe get yourself into unnecessary trouble.

TOP TIP!

Always show the utmost respect for any authority you meet, but always maintain your rights, and never let your documents 'disappear', because you may find that to make them 'reappear' it'll cost you money... so beware.

Patience. Always be patient. You have all the time in the world, so getting angry or being rude will get you absolutely nowhere... in fact it'll normally get you further away from what you hope to achieve than in the first place. You could therefore be left waiting for hours at border crossings for example. It's funny really, because sometimes as a backpacker you are seen as harmless and so at things like border crossings you are rushed through fairly quickly. However sometimes this is not the case, and you find yourself being checked, double checked, searched, etc. The secret is to be as clean and tidy as possible. If you have one of those backpacks where you can zip away all the straps, etc. and carry the bag horizontally like a holdall, all the better. Men, have a shave. Women, if you have long hair, wash it, wear it neatly, and already be dressed in accordance with any rules that the country has... get those legs covered up before you have to be dragged aside and told to do it. I know it can be a bit unfair on you, but at least you're only visiting and don't have to live like that every day, eh?

Photos. Cameras can be a real pain in the arse. If you have a really good one, make sure that it is insured. However having too good a camera may attract the wrong sort of attention, and so may make you unnecessarily on guard too much of the time. If it is too big, you might find it awkward, heavy and bulky. However it you have a cheap one the picture quality may not be as good. Not having a zoom lens meant that I have missed out on some great photos... ..I have been with in spitting distance of bears, moose, killer whales, etc., but have no decent photos as with my camera they all seem to be miles away. So unless the thing is actually sitting on my lap, I just don't expect to get a good photo. If I could do it all again I would invest in one of those compact little numbers that has a zoom lens on it. They are now becoming cheaper and cheaper as technology improves, and so if you can afford to, why not invest in one of them? Remember that once you have finished your trip, which will go a lot quicker than expected, the photos will become a big reminder of your trip. One of my biggest regrets is not having a decent camera as I have missed out on some great once in a lifetime photos, as well as many others not coming out.

Disposable cameras. Have you ever used or thought about using these? Having had my camera dropped in the sea on the Barrier Reef in Australia, it decided it had had enough of my maltreatment of it, and so decided to give up its fight for life! We were then forced to use disposable cameras. They are actually relatively cheap, and the photos that come out really aren't bad at all. I wouldn't recommend them for the whole duration of your trip as it would be cheaper to have a decent camera. However for certain events during your trip they are a great idea. The waterproof ones are great if you go diving, and I've got some ace piccies of me snorkelling on the Barrier Reef. They are also useful and robust enough to take out to beach parties, on any night out, whilst trekking, and generally on anything that you might do where the camera might get thrown around a bit. On these type of events you can share the cost of buying and developing with a group of friends, allowing you to get some class memorable photos at an affordable price. So if you're all off to some major event that you want to have photos of, arm yourself with one, and split the costs.

Question: Do you develop your photos as you go along?

- If you do you can write everybody's names, comments, etc. on the back... instead of waiting until you get home, forgetting, and possibly not getting them all down.
- If you don't it may mean that you literally have hundreds to sort out when you get home, which you may never do... I still haven't done any of mine, and they are now all sitting loose in a box, muddled and in a helluva mess. I think it would take about a week now to get them sorted.
- Getting them developed as you go along will mean that you will spread the cost of development over time, rather than having a massive bill when you finally do get them done.
- However if you do get them developed then you have to carry them around with you... they can be heavy, bulky, and may well get damaged.
- But then if you carry your films around with you, you will have to look after them really well to stop them getting wet/damaged! It has also been known for some X Ray machines to wipe the films, however you can get X Ray bags to protect them when they go through. To be sure, get them checked by hand as you go through.

So what do you reckon is the best thing to do? Tony and I actually sent our films home in a package of things from Australia. A good idea, but a risky one, as I'd have been gutted if they had got lost in the post.

Well, each to their own, you just have to do what you think is the best for you.

Photography.

- Should be done with all care and consideration.

- Some people may not like cameras being stuck in their faces, to others it may be considered bad luck as some believe that it takes their spirit away.

- Always ask their permission, and don't push it if they say no, as you'll only end up with your Canon 35mm telephoto lens, great camera, ace photos... bouncing from rock to rock as it finds its own way to the bottom of the canyon!

- Never offer money in exchange for taking a photo. As indicated elsewhere in the book, this may lead to offence, and may also set a precedent for everyone else.

- Politeness, smiles and a bit of cunning will get you all of those unusual photos that you want.

- Try to avoid letting locals take photos of you with your camera. A nice gesture... yes, it usually is. But you may find that one time you will give it to the wrong person who has the speed of Linford Christie, the slipperiness of a snake, and the hiding powers of a golf ball in the Arctic, and who answers to the name of 'Toccohamayeea' ('The Shadow'). Meanwhile at the police station (as you need the report for the insurance)... "Well he was an Indonesian male, about 5'5', sandals, black trousers, white shirt, black hair, and also answered to the name of 'Made'" (the name given to every first born male). So with only about 4 million people to choose from... your camera has gone!

DAD'S TOP TIP!

Tom's

PIN Numbers. If you have credit cards and all sorts of other PIN numbers that you need to remember, here's quite a handy way of being able to have it written down and secure at the same time.

On the back of a card of some sort write down in order all the letters of the alphabet from A–Z. Then pick some four letter word that you will remember such as 'BLAG' (a friend of mine Steve's nickname – amongst others!). Then put your pin number under those letters in that order, and then fill in all the other letters with other numbers:

My PIN is 8279 (it's not in case you try and nick my card... even I'm not that dumb!!)

A	B	C	D	E	F	G	H	I	J	K	L	M	N	O	P	Q	R	S	T	U	V	W	X	Y	Z
7	8	0	3	4	9	9	1	46	2	2	4	8	5	1	0	3	37	5	8	1		3	8	2	

Visa and Access   **Steve Freeman**

Police. Always go to them if you have any trouble or problems, especially if in Westernised countries. However it is in certain corrupt developing countries that you may have to treat them with a little bit of caution. Yes there are loads of stories that do the rounds about the police in places like Mexico taking your passport from you and then basically 'mugging' you of your money to get it back. I've personally never had any problems, however a couple of my friends have… just be aware of some of the 'tricky things' that they might get up to. Some undercover police have been known to offer drugs to backpackers, arrest them, and then blackmail them of their money so that they don't spend time in a foreign prison. All nasty stuff I'm sure you will agree.

However in places like Thailand, I'm all in favour of the Thai Tourist Police. Wanting to get rid of the image of being blackmailers and rip-off merchants, the Tourist Police now have the powers to go into clubs, shops and bars, and quite literally… kick arse! If you have any problems you can go straight to them, as they have the power to close places down. In most places the police are very efficient, so do use them. But if in doubt, get in touch with the Embassy first. Usually 'The tourist is always right', so play on it!

Protection.

♦ The little alarms that you can get over here, you know the ones that I mean, the rape alarms that are issued to women… they are class, and great for your own protection and peace of mind. Having lived in Manchester for 3 years, I think that women should get used to carrying them around.

♦ They are nifty little things, small and not very heavy… but most importantly, they do their job. To an unsuspecting attacker they would give them a serious shock, and so give you the time to get away. They are also great for attracting attention.

TOP TIP!

Never shout 'Help!', always shout 'Fire!' when in need of help, as you are more likely to get a response. True fact.

♦ But they are not only for women. You may think that as a bloke you are hard, macho, and beyond being attacked/mugged. I think you've been reading too many comics, lads! It can happen to anyone, so you don't have to feel a soft shite if you carry one in your backpack… you never know when it might come in handy.

Some are activated by having a chord pulled out, and are designed so that they can be attached to doors at night... if you feel uneasy, attach it to the door, and if it is opened, the alarm goes off.

Similarly, you can wander around with the chord round your wrist, and the alarm in your bag. If the bag is snatched, the thief is left with a piercing alarm to get rid of (and so will usually drop the bag and run off).

As for self protection, I'm a great believer on thinking on your feet, doing the unexpected, and outsmarting any would be attacker. I have evaded mugging twice, simply by walking straight out in the middle of the road amongst the traffic which gave them a bit of a shock, and the second time I pretended to be a 'Manc' with a fake Manc accent... put doubt in the bloke's mind and gave me valuable time to get away. Another great one I have heard is of a woman in an underground car park by herself... she saw a couple of dodgy blokes in between her and her car. She couldn't be sure as to their intentions, so she put her arms up like an aeroplane and then 'flew' to her car making aeroplane noises. They thought she was crazy... she was safe. There's no point in getting embarrassed about it, you just have to do whatever comes in to your head, something unexpected, and then just get out of there.

☛ *However, do use judgement between adventure and stupidity, assess the situation first.*

☛ *Why not take a quick self defence class before you go, there are loads of them about at all the local sports centres, etc. Well, why not? You never know when a few techniques might come in handy some day.*

Plastic bags. Don't stand out as a tourist with a backpack, map, camera an sombrero! By going for a wander around town with your things in a plai plastic bag, you'll make yourself look ordinary, part of the scene, and so wi naturally blend in. Placcy B's also great for storing wet things in withou making everything else in your bag wet too.

Queen. You may be asked many times 'How is she?' 'She's fine!' normall does the trick, unless of course you know her personally, where a tru account of her well being might be in order. On no account pretend to be a member of the Royal Family unless you are an exceptional blagger, or if i may lead to fantastic hospitality and a lot of wealth coming your way. I thin it is still classed as Treason and will be frowned upon by the Government the Royal Family, and your host if ever you are found out.

Similarly with Queen the group... in places thousands of miles from home claiming an association with the band or the late Freddie Mercury accompanied by a few badly sung versions of their classics, will possibly get you a long way. In fact this is a great blag to play with any famous person- ality, because by the time they find out that Paul McCartney never had a son called Tom, I'll be thousands of miles away anyway!

Rules. All countries have them, whether they are to do with religion, drugs, dress codes, festivals, litter, behaviour, drinking, etc. Make an effort to find out what they are in the countries that you are visiting, and do try and stick to them. Denying knowledge of them will only get you so far, and some- times nowhere at all (unless you are caught 'Jaywalking' in America... "What is 'Jaywalking' old chap, back in England we cross the roads where we like"... usually gets you off, but may not!).

Shipping/Posting items. Sending things back home can be a great idea. If you find that you have too much stuff, putting a little package together and sending it home is one of the best solutions. If you have been to all the cold countries that you are going to, why not send those heavy jumpers back through the post. The obvious problem is them never reaching the destina- tion. I have seen the best of all the angles... ..everything from sending things by air (which can be very expensive, but at least you know that it's got more chance of getting there), to sending it overland. This is the cheaper way, and indeed a package that we sent back from Australia did make it. It was quite a dodgy thing to do looking back on it as it had all of our films in it to date, and all those bits and pieces that were irreplaceable, such as my bungy video and photos. However they got there. But, having nearly killed myself in the heat trying to get a present in the post for my brother Mat's birthday from Fiji, I was gutted to find that it never turned up. It probably never left the island, and may even have ended up back in the shop where I bought it, who knows?

Ship items home sir? Many shops may offer to ship souvenirs back home for you in order to get a sale. Yes this can work very well, however call me Mr. Sceptical at the thought of countless items that have got 'lost in the post' but mysteriously never leave the shelf in the shop… it's a long way to go back to ask why they took the money and never posted the damn thing!

Sleeping in airports/bus stations, etc. Sometimes you may find that this is a good idea if you have a very early bus or plane. It would mean that you wouldn't have to pay for a night's accommodation that you don't really use, and you don't have to get up even earlier to go and catch the flight. The natural worry is going to sleep, waking up, and finding all your belongings gone. If worried, try to sleep 'entangled' in your backpack, or if you have a small chain, chain your pack to the seat. In decent airports you shouldn't have to worry, as there is usually ample security around to watch over you anyway. Beware, it can get very cold even in the hottest of countries, as without the doors constantly opening and closing, the air conditioning works overtime and creates nice Arctic conditions. I experienced this in Brisbane airport and had one of the most uncomfortable nights in my life, wrapped up in about three T Shirts, jeans, towels, etc… not very pleasant!

Sleeping bags. Make sure that you have the best possible sleeping bag for the climates that you are going to come up against. If you aren't sure, go to the camping shops and ask their advice (and remember the voucher in the back for Millets). The sleeping bag that I use is a tiny two season one that packs away to nothing. In hot countries it is great, as when it is really hot at night I simply lie on it unzipped. The problem is that when it does get fairly cold it is absolutely bugger all use, forcing me to sleep in loads of clothes inside it. The dilemma you'll probably face is how thick a one can you buy, and how small will it pack down to. You can buy little compactor bags that you stuff the sleeping bag in to and then pull the toggles to compact it down even more, and which I believe work very well. With a thicker sleeping bag you do have an advantage in that you are warmer when it gets cold, and when it gets hot you'll simply sleep on top of it anyway.

- Do shop around and get what you think is best for you. Do think about the weight of it, and how much space it will take up in your pack, as this will start to become quite important as your pack gets fuller and fuller.
- Try to air the sleeping bag as often as you can, as it will tend to sweat and start to smell after a while.
- Remember that you are going to have to get at it virtually every day, so think about this when you are doing your final pack. If your pack has a separate bottom compartment this is ideal.
- Remember also that in most hostels they require you to have a sleeping sheet, so make sure you get one. The sleeping sheets that are sewn up to give a 'sleeping bag effect' are very useful in that they can give you an extra layer of warmth when it is cold, but you can also fill them with your clothes (and valuables if you want) and use it as a pillow.

☞ **Think about it! Use judgement between adventure and stupidity.**

Tourist Information booths. Great places, full of information, but hardly ever used! Why not? They'll be able to tell you the cheapest and safest way to get around, the best deals, etc. They'll also supply you with maps, other useful information, where to go, and more importantly, where not to go. If they're there, use them. I really don't understand why people have an aversion to them, one of the mysteries of this world!

Touts. In every country they'll always be around to prey on the baffled and bewildered tourists. They will always offer the best deals and often rip you off. Beat them by being confident and prepared. They won't hang around you if you look as though you know what you are doing. By being bold and assertive you can 'play the game'... and win!

Trains/buses/local transport. At each stop, keep an eye on your baggage and make sure that it doesn't get off until you decide to (as quite often it will be stored in the compartment under the bus and so could easily be removed without your knowledge... which is another good reason to take off all identifying labels from the outside).

Train compartments. Make sure that you lock the door if you are sleeping in a separate one, as tourists are quite vulnerable when on trains. Don't be put off by the stories of the French/Russian bandits chloroforming people in their sleep... yes it did happen in about 1990, but it was a very rare case. And besides if it did happen you wouldn't know about it until you wake up and it would be all over. In short, more chance of having an intelligent conversation with a constipated kitten than it happening to you.

Universities. Some are now asking for an indication of a plan that you might have for your year off before deciding to interview. They will want to know that you will be getting something useful out of it and not just going off to bum around for a bit until you have a decent suntan. So make it good but not bullshitty.

Vegetarians. If you let the airlines know that you are vegetarian when you book the tickets or before you get on the plane, you will normally get the vegetarian meal. The benefits are that they are normally quite good and you will usually be served first. Be aware of your diet, make sure that you get enough protein, etc. in your day to day diet. Eating loads of things like bananas, nuts, and fruit for your Vitamin C should keep you nice and healthy. However, due to the general fear amongst backpackers of dodgy meat in various areas of the world, you'll find that your ranks will swell considerably!

Wildlife. The great myth is that all wildlife will come and attack you. Yet if you think about it, we are a species of 'wildlife' – would you, if you saw a cow walking near you, go and attack it? Would it attack you? Exactly. I know there are a lot of exceptions in that snakes, bears and crocodiles are slightly more dangerous than the odd cow, but the point is that if you make loads of noise then even dangerous animals will move away to avoid a confrontation. If you startle them, some may attack, so by making plenty of noise in forests and long grassy areas, things like snakes won't sit around and wait to be trodden on. However when in hibernation season, exceptions have to be made to the noise making rule! Being brought up in the UK, the majority of us are totally unused to wildlife, therefore whilst camping and trekking in areas all over the world it is always a good idea to find out what the locals think about the surrounding wildlife, and digest any tips that they have for you.

Bears for example. Did you know that they can run faster than racehorses, swim faster then Duncan Goodhew and Sharon Davis put together, and can climb trees? Having been brought up on Yogi Bear and Gentle Ben, I was under the impression that I would be able to get away from this big lumbering creature. Guess I was wrong, eh? As for taking one on with a couple of quick Frank Bruno jabs to the head... a fully grown Grizzly can take the head off a moose with just one swipe! Makes you feel pretty vulnerable.

☞ *Wildlife... if you respect it, it will respect you!*

CHAPTER 13

Coming Home

'The more I see of other countries the more I love my own.'
Anna Louis de Stael 1807.

A few final words on the subject of travel

Just to round this little book off. Yes, you will have changed, and for the better I hope. However, don't push this point. I know that I have mentioned it a few times, but it is something that you should notice in yourself, and which others will notice in you. However don't become the 'smart arse traveller' and start pointing this out to everyone who comes near... you'll do yourself no favours. But I'm sure you're not like that anyway.

You will undoubtedly come across a few problems with friends, even ones that you have had for years. You will find that although you have changed, be it in a big or small way, everyone else is exactly the same as when you left, depending of course on age group, job, college, family commitments, etc. Beware – don't be a travel bore, as it is very easy to slip into. BUT on the other hand, be proud of what you have done and achieved. You must remember that everyone has the chance to do something like this in their life, 99% don't... but you have. Off the cuff remarks from many, usually disguised in jokes aimed at causing you discomfort, is only really jealousy coming out.

Traveller's tales!

You will find that the people that are genuinely interested in where you have gone, and what you have been up to will make themselves clear to you. It is with these that you will be able to share a few of the great things that happened during your trip. A lot of things will happen to you while you are away. Many of them will be amazing things that you will never have even come close to experiencing before. They may have blown your mind, and still give you a great feeling when you think of them. They will also be in the forefront of your mind, and so in general conversation with your mates, whilst words trigger off thoughts to them of a programme that they saw last week on the television, the same words trigger memories of you white water rafting in Africa... and you really want to tell them just how much you 'peed your pants'! This is not your fault, just because you have had a bit of adventure in your life. You will then be barracked by calls of 'travellers tales again!' Unfortunately I did get this quite a lot at one point. I can take a joke like the rest of them, but it just happened to go on too much, to the point that I got it the whole time. You must put your foot down, otherwise you may get frustrated and start regretting that you have travelled, something which you must never do.

It's a narrow minded world after all!

With new broadened horizons you will undoubtedly start to find people a bit narrow minded in a few of their views. I am not being 'yeah well man… I mean… as a traveller man… you have the forefront knowledge of the world at your fingertips man', as you will have more than gathered now that I'm totally the opposite of that. Do you remember that at the start I made the point of people settling down into their own little worlds that revolve solely around them? This really is true, and it happens in the end to everybody.

You only have to look at America to find a population of narrow minded people. You may think… he's off again, fasten your seatbelts, he's about to have a go at 'Yanks' again. But the thing is that even American academics point to the fall down of Americans in that they are a very insular people, which makes them extremely narrow minded. On their 'Prime Time News', all you hear about is America. And then you have the Trevor McDonald of the 'show' saying… 'and finally, over a million people are feared dead in Rwanda, Africa, and the Europeans are up in arms again about some silly little war atrocities in Yugoslavia, Europe… I hope Princess Diana is alright!' They are so uninformed about the world in general that it is no surprise that I and my friends have been asked questions like 'Do you have any rivers in England?', 'How long does it take to get a train from your country to ours?', 'How many days of the week do you have over there?' These are genuine questions that we have been asked… something that makes me really despair of the most powerful nation in the world. I have somewhat detracted from the point I was making, but I'm sure that you are used to that by now!

More employable?… well, I think so!

I believe that when I left to go travelling for the first time, I was a very naive and cocky 18 year old, and narrow minded like the rest. Since coming back, and indeed since travelling some more, I believe that I am a bit more broad minded about a lot more things. I do believe that I am more employable, and in fact many employers are more than happy to interview people who have had a year off and gone travelling, as they are seen as more broad minded in their views. You will have more to put on your CV's and application forms, and a lot to talk about in your interviews.

A lot of the jobs that I am applying for at the moment have about 3,000 applications. If you think about how big a pile of 3,000 applications is, you will realise the enormity of the job of selection. What many companies will do is give the whole lot to a clerk, and ask them to sift out all the unqualified ones. Having done this they will ask the clerk to turn to the hobbies/interests section, and have a flick through. If in their 5 second flick through they see something of interest, it will be kept. If not… see ya, game over. Why? Well, because if you can't interest a clerk, then who can you interest? Things of interest: travelling the world, bungy jumping, rafting, sailing, funny events that happened. No interest: doing gymnastics at the age of 12, being a member of the school chess club at 14, and winning a Blue Peter badge for a magnificent 'Bring and Buy' sale that you organised in your garage in 1989 which raised £64.72. And remember that everyone 'plays sport' and 'enjoys reading' and 'likes to socialise'. Everyone is also 'highly ambitious' and 'likes to succeed'... but what gives you the qualification to be able to say this?

What they want is evidence that you have a life!

Why are you different from the rest? Why should you be of more interest to them than the next person? Why? Because you have got off your backside and done something that you have wanted to do... and had a ball doing it.

Having undertaken a 'big trip' of some sort you will have exhibited signs of confidence, organisation, planning, decision making, financial control, possibly decisions under pressure, leadership/teamwork skills, etc. Do you get this from 'enjoy reading'?

From the strength of my CV and application forms I would like to think that I can get straight to the interview stage. I have in the past, and so things now should be no different. I'm not being the 'Big I AM' here, I'm just stating a fact. I have confidence about what I write about myself, a position that many don't find themselves in at our age. Because I have got off my arse and done what I want to in my life, I do have a lot to talk about. Unfortunately I have not been suitable for any of the work I have gone for... so far, but I know soon that things are going to change.

Margaret Murray, Head of the CBI's Education Policy Group: 'Travel is thought to be a good idea if it gives the young person the 'oomph' to start work. But it is not the sort of travel where you wander around the world with a rucksack dreaming. If a young person can answer the question 'What has been achieved as a result of the year?' then we would be interested in interviewing them.' All I have to say to Ms Murray is that she illustrates what I have just been sprouting on about perfectly, and if she would like to read my book... I am available for interview any time!

Itchy feet

When you come back you may find it difficult to fit back into the old routine for a while, and those itchy feet won't be happy unless they're under a backpack in a strange country thousands of miles from home... 'largeing it up' on a tropical beach, or on the edge of a volcano, in a raging river, or on the steps of one of the wonders of the world! (I'm only saying this to whet your appetite and make you want to go even more!). In fact, I even think to myself, why am I sitting here in this computer room in Suffolk College, type

type type type type all day (often wondering what the brunette's name is sitting to the left of me!) when I could be off travelling somewhere? But then I go to the bank and realise why I still am here, and shatter all my dreams. This is something that I am going to rectify in the very near future though.

However for the moment, my memories which accompany me all the time while I'm typing are enough for a simple young pup like myself! But you will fit back in to it all; after all, this is your country and your culture... except with tastes of different cultures, you may be a bit more 'cultured' now. Don't bore your friends, don't alienate them, and don't be alienated by them. 'When I was in Australia... ', 'Oh yeah, when I was in Thailand...' You'll stick out like a punk at a reggae concert, but you will be the last person to realise this. Jealousy can be cruel but will fade away, self satisfaction and fantastic memories can't be beaten, and will be around forever.

Goodbye and Good Luck

OK, well that's about all from me, I'll take up your time no longer. My aim in this book is to produce something that will be of use to everyone who reads it. Everyone seems to talk about money... will I make any, how much, etc., etc. The truth is that I really don't know, and to be honest I really don't care. I am 22 years old, and at the moment I have no job. I am financing myself by digging into my student loans. Yeah, financially I could be doing better, but the thing is that I am ecstatically happy with my life... how many people can say that?.

I have had my struggles like everyone else, and at the time of writing the struggle with my Dad still goes on. In a way this book is really dedicated to him, as I hope that he realises that I am an adult now, and that I am in control of my own life. At present I am achieving goals and ambitions. I love it! I hope that one day he will be able to turn round and tell me that yes, he is proud of me. But until that day, my life goes on.

I will always strive to get the most out of my life, and enjoy it as only I know how... by living every day and every opportunity to the full. I strive to be 'larger than life', and my hope is that you will too. I want this book to be of use to every potential young backpacker out there. The world is out there. Why not live your dreams? What is stopping you?... well Jack Buggery really! So do it, go for it, and have a great time. The fact that you are at this point in the book means that you are about to go anyway, so I'll hold you up no longer. All I say is Good Luck, and do send me a postcard if you like, as I'd love to hear how you are getting on (via publishers address page iv).

Things to do Check-list

OK, a little organisation doesn't do anyone any harm, and in fact you may find that it does in fact do you a bit of good. There are a lot of things that you have to remember, other things that you may not realise have to be done... and if you have a memory like mine, you're going to need to note a few things down somewhere. Normally I get a little notebook to note times, appointments, meetings, etc., down. This is much better than the old system of writing these things on pieces of paper, and having them loose on the desk in my room. Hence I forgot about doctor's appointments, to pick up travellers cheques, and a few other mundane things that have to be done.

So I thought about what would be of use to you, and have tried to make something that really is of use to you. Anything related to the preparation for your trip can be noted down in the next few pages, so you can keep everything together, and find it all at a glance. It really is worth doing you know, so give it a go! I've tried to put some sort of order into the list, so you don't find that you've got a couple of days until take off, and absolutely shed loads left to do. Plan early, and everything will run smoothly.

When things are done, why not cross them out with a thick pen so that the things left to do are clear to see?

Are you sure you want to go travelling?

❑ **Yes (carry on)**   ❑ **No (Liar... carry on!)**

Do you know where you want to go?

❑ **Yes**   ❑ **No (Go to Travel Agents)**

TRAVEL AGENTS
Which are your nearest travel agents?

When you have some time free, call in to a travel agents and pick up all the brochures that you think might be applicable. Dream for a while, about what you think you might like to do, and where you might like to go. The brochures are class, as they are full of all those glossy pictures that you really want to see. This is the very first step that will get you in the mood. Take them home, and spend a weekend, or a couple of days flicking through them, looking at the pictures, and seeing the places you would like to visit. Take the STA Travel challenge! For your nearest one, see the back of the book. It really is worth your while... I wouldn't be wasting my time saying it otherwise!

Set a day to visit the best ones ___/___/___ Don't forget to ask about their best deals, insurance, visas, itineraries, injections, and anything else you want to know. Take your time asking all the questions, and let them sell you the best deal they can possibly give you.

What are the 3 best trips offered?
The 3 best Insurance deals?
Do you need Visas?
For which countries?
Available before you go?
When do you think that you may go? ___/___/___
Where do you think that you may go?

Who are you going with? Unsure? Tough decision to make I know. However in these situations it is better to be cruel to be kind. If you really think that it is a bad idea going with someone in particular, don't ruin a friendship by going with them, only to fall out half way around the world. You will also ruin your trip.

☞ *Still in doubt? Why not re-read 'Going with a friend'?*

MEDICAL / HEALTH
Arrange a Doctor's appointment ASAP.

Good to have a check up before you go.
Date of appointment __/__/__
Don't forget to discuss

♦ regular medicine you may take
♦ the Pill, and other contraception queries (free condoms at family planning)
♦ allergies
♦ travel sickness (if you suffer from it)
♦ any other questions. Don't be shy... it's better to ask now than to regret not asking about something, whilst necking the free beer they keep throwing at you on the plane, wishing that you had, and trying to forget about it
♦ getting a note about any drugs that you may have to take with you.

your appendix. Is it still in? If it is, ask:
- where is it located
- what pains are associated with appendicitis
- how to diagnose that you have it
- what to do

Do you need injections?
Date of injections ___/___/___
Any further injections? Date ___/___/___

Do you start a course of tablets e.g. Malaria?
The course starts ___/___/___
To be taken every _____

BUYING THE TICKET
Total cost, including insurance, and any other bits £
When do you need to buy it by? ___/___/___
What date are you actually going? ___/___/___
Do you have to give notice for work? By what date? ___/___/___

FINANCES
How much do you need to take? £
Are you going to try and budget?
If so, how much a day/week/month? £
Do you need advice from the bank?
On foreign exchange, travellers cheques, money transfer, credit cards, or any other matters that you need help with.
Meeting arranged for ___/___/___
Are you taking an International Debit Card?
Do you need to order one?
Does the one you have need replacing?
Do you need to organise Money Transfer?
Signing your account over to your parents?
A very good idea; go to the bank and sign the forms.
Travellers cheques, do you have to order them? Date? ___/___/___
When are you picking them up? ___/___/___
Is everything up to date/have the correct address on?
♦ Passport
♦ Credit cards
♦ Injections
♦ Overdraft
♦ E111 (if going to Europe)

Don't get caught out with your cards, passport, etc. expiring whilst you are travelling. It is a major hassle, one which you really don't need. It is also very pointless, as if you have done all the proper checks before you go, then it needn't happen.

Time to photocopy everything! (Tick)

Passport

Insurance certificates

Travellers Cheques

Airline Tickets

Credit Cards and Emergency Numbers

Evidence of Jabs/Blood Group/Sanity!

References

Medical documents

Evidence of qualifications (GCSE's, 'A' Levels, Degree etc.)

Anything else you consider important

While you're at this stage, do extra copies for yourself to carry in your pack and your day bag, and while you remember, go and give the other copies to your parents/friends with all the relevant instructions.

CLOTHES

What do you need to buy?
Can you borrow anything?
Is your Birthday/Christmas before you go?

What items could you get as presents?

Remember that this is a great way to get all those little bits and pieces that you would like to have, but which you really can't afford. Let your relatives help you out, or any one else who wants to for that matter! However only get things that you need and not things that *they* think you need!

Any accessories that you really need?

Do you really need them, or are they just going to clog up your backpack? If you think that you may not need it, then you probably don't.

FINAL PREPARATION

At this point take in to account things like

- Packing, re-packing, and final packing
- Picking up tickets
- Picking up money
- Organising a lift to the airport/station
- Getting addresses
- Photocopying documents
- Picking up medication
- Ensuring travel partner(s) are just as ready as you. If they aren't... kick their arse into gear!
- Sorting out final arrangements/questions of parents
- Time for a farewell party that won't leave you so knackered and hungover that you are in no fit state to do any of the above.
- Cursing me for making it sound so easy!

7 DAYS TO GO   __/__/__

6 DAYS TO GO   __/__/__

5 DAYS TO GO   __/__/__

4 DAYS TO GO   __/__/__

3 DAYS TO GO   __/__/__

2 DAYS TO GO   __/__/__

1 DAY TO GO   __/__/__

Why not write out a big plan like this to note down all the vital last minute things so you don't forget them?

D – DAY... YOU'RE OFF, HAVE A GREAT TIME!

Good books on the market

Travelling Accounts
BBC *More Great Railway Journeys*
Ffyona Campbell *Feet of Clay* – her epic walk across Australia
Ffyona Campbell *On Foot Through Africa*
Ffyona Campbell *The Whole Story*
Nick Danziger *Danziger's Adventures*
Nick Danziger *Danziger's Travels*
Josie Dew *Travels in a Strange State - Cycling across the USA*
Kuki Gallmann *I Dreamed of Africa*
Traveller's Eye A Trail of Visions
Howard Jacobson *In the Land of Oz*
Irma Kutz *The Great American Bus Ride*
Matthew Parris *Inca – Kola A traveller's tale of Peru*
Mark Tully *The Heart of India*
Ronald Wright *Time Among the Maya - Travels in Belize, Guatamala, and Mexico*

Novels
Maria Coffey *Three Moons in Vietnam*
Michael Crichton *Travels*
Jack Kerouac *On the Road*
Jane Robinson *Unsuitable for Ladies - An anthology of women travellers*
Jon Swain *River of Time (Indo China)*
Paul Theroux *The Pillars of Hercules*
(plus many more books if you like this author)

Humorous Travelling Accounts
Bill Bryson *Made in America*
Bill Bryson *Neither Here Nor There*
Bill Bryson *Notes From a Small Island*
Bill Bryson *The Lost Continent*
Billy Connolly *World Tour of Australia*
Joseph O'Connor *The Irish Male – at home and abroad*
P.J O'Rourke *Holidays in Hell*
Michael Palin *Around the World in 80 Days*
Michael Palin *Pole to Pole*

Informative Travel
Tom Griffiths *Before You Go*
John Hatt *The Tropical Traveller*
May Morris *Nothing to Declare: Memoirs of a Woman Travelling Alone*
Rough Guides *Women Travel*
Rough Guide Special *More Women Travel*
Weather to Travel The Traveller's Guide to the World's Weather

Travel Guides
Lonely Planet (covers just about every country on the planet!)

Year Off Information
A Year Off… A Year On – Hobsons Publishing, A CRAC Publication (01223) 354 551
Work Your Way Around The World Susan Griffith (01865) 241 978
The Gap Year Guidebook. Peridot Press
A Year Between: The Complete Guide to Taking a Year Out
Central Bureau for Educational Visits and Exchanges (0171) 725 9402
Working Holidays

APPENDIX 3

Useful addresses and telephone numbers

Travel Agencies
STA Travel (0171) 361 6161 Europe
(0171) 361 6262 Worldwide
http://www.statravel.co.uk
Trailfinders (0171) 937 5499

Travel Guides
Lonely Planet (0181) 742 3161
http://www.lonelyplanet.com.au
Travel and Travel Handbooks (01225)
469 141
ISIC Helpline (0181) 666 9205 A 24
hour service for travelling ISIC Card
holders. Whatever your enquiry, they're
there to help (*see* end of book).

Voluntary Work
AFS The American Free Service
Arden House, Wellington Street, Bingley,
West Yorkshire BD16 2NB. Tel: (01274)
560 677 Fax: (01274) 567 675. *Live with
a family for 6 months – 1 year, learn a lan-
guage, and work on social projects in Brazil,
Colombia, and Honduras.*
BUNAC The British Universities North
America Club. *£4 membership gives you
access to the organisation's work programmes
in America, Australia, and Canada.*
Tel: (0171) 251 3472
GAP Activity Projects. *An educational
charity that organises voluntary work in
more than 30 countries. £25 to register +*

*£420 placement fee + pay for flights, insur-
ance, etc. Get free board + pocket money.*
Tel: (01734) 594 914
GAP Challenge World Challenge
Expeditions. *3 – 6 month work placements
as teachers/social workers. Cost £1,200.
Includes training, accomodation, and return
flight.* Tel: (0181) 961 1122
Project Trust *At least 9 months voluntary
work posts. Best apply 1 year in advance, 1
week selection course. Costs £2,950.* Tel:
(01879) 230 444
VSO Voluntary Services Overseas
317, Putney Bridge Road, London SW15
2PN. Tel: (0181) 780 2266 or (0181) 780
1331 – 24 hour answerphone
http://www.oneworld.org/vso/

Government Advice Numbers
British Embassy (0171) 273 3000
Foreign Office Travel Advice (0171) 270
4129. (0374) 500 900 For recorded
information
Foreign and Commenwealth Office
(0171) 270 1500 – 24 hour, first contact
number. (0171) 238 4503/4504 – Travel
Advice Unit. http://www.fco.gov.uk/
Health Advice for Travellers 0800 555
777 For a free booklet
HM Customs & Excise Advice Centre
(0171) 202 4227
Home Office – Drug/Medication

Questions (0171)273 3806
London School of Tropical Medicine
Medical advice for travellers on (0171) 631 4408
Passport Enquiries (0990)210 410
BBC Ceefax p.470 onwards: up-to-date information on safety in more than 130 countries

Would you like Sponsorship?

Rotary International (0171) 487 5429
Lions Club International (01245) 813 661
Round Table (0121) 456 4402
Chamber of Commerce (0171) 248 4444
Students applications must explain what they hope to achieve in their gap year.

Motoring

Automobile Association (01256) 20123
Royal Automobile Club (0345) 33 11 33

Tourist Boards

English Tourist Board (0181) 846 9000
N.Ireland Tourist Board (01232) 246 609
Scottish Tourist Board (0131) 332 2433
Welsh Tourist Board (01222) 499 909

Airports

Aberdeen (01224) 722 331
Belfast (City) (01232) 45 77 45
Belfast (Inter) (01849) 422 888
Birmingham (0121) 767 5511
Bristol (01275) 474 444
Cardiff (01446) 711 111
East Midlands (01332) 852 852
Edinburgh (0131) 333 1000
Gatwick (01293) 53 53 53
Glasgow (0141) 887 1111
Heathrow (0181) 759 4321
Liverpool (0151) 486 8877
Luton (01582) 405 100
Manchester (0161) 489 3000
Newcastle (0191) 286 0966
Stansted (01279) 680 500
Swansea (01792) 204 063
Teesside (01325) 332 811
Republic of Ireland Cork
  00 325 21 31 31 31
Dublin 00 353 18 444 900

Ferry Ports and Operators

Dover (Stena Sealink) (01304) 242 818
Felixstowe (P&O) (0990) 980 980
Folkstone (Le Shuttle) (0990) 35 35 35
Harwich (Scandinavian Seaways)
  (01255) 240 240
Hoverspeed (01304) 240 241
Newhaven (Stena Sealink)
  (01273) 364 099
Portsmouth (Brittany Ferries)
  (01705) 827 701
Ramsgate (Sally Line) (01843) 595 522
Weymouth (Condor Ferries)
  (01305) 761 551

Religious Festivals and Anniversaries

Christian-Western

	1997		1998	
Ash Wednesday	February	12	February	25
Quadragesima	February	16	March	1
Palm Sunday	March	23	April	5
Good Friday	March	28	April	10
Easter Day	March	30	April	12
Ascension Day	May	8	May	21
Whit Sunday	May	18	May	31
Trinity Sunday	May	25	June	7
Advent Sunday	November	30	November	29
Christmas Day	December	25	December	25

Roman Catholic Holy Days of Obligation

	1997		1998	
Epiphany (England/Wales)				
Epiphany (Ireland)	January	5	January	6
St Patrick (Ireland)	January	6	January	6
Ascension	March	17	March	17
Corpus Christi (England/Wales, Ireland)	May	8	May	21
St Peter and St Paul (England/Wales)	May	29	June	11
St Peter and St Paul (Scotland, Ireland)	June	29	June	28
Assumption (England/Wales)	June	29	June	29#
Assumption (Scotland, Ireland)	August	15	August	16
All Saints (England/Wales, Scotland)	August	15	August	15#
All Saints (Ireland)	November	1#	November	1
Immaculate Conception (Ireland)	November	2	November	1
Christmas Day	December	8	December	8
	December	25	December	25

obligation dispensed in Scotland

Buddhist

	1997		1998	
Paranirvana Day				
Wesak Day	February	15	February	15
Dharma Day	May	22	May	11
	July	20	July	9

Chinese

	1997		1998	
Lunar New Year	February	7-9	January	28-30

Christian-Eastern Orthodox

	1997		1998	
Christmas (not Greek Orthodox)	January	7	January	7
Lent Monday	March	10	March	2
Easter Day	April	27	April	19
Pentecost	June	15	June	7

Hindu

	1997		1998	
Holi	March	23	March	12
Navratri	October	2	September	21
Diwali	October	30	October	19
New Year	November	1	October	21

Islamic (dates subject to visibility of new moon at Mecca)

	A.H. 1417		A.H. 1718	
1st of Ramadan	January	10	-	
Eid-Al-Fittr	February	8	January	29
Eid-Al-Addha	April	17	April	7
	A.H. 1418		A.H. 1419	
Al Hijra (New Year)	May	7	-	
Ashura	May	16	-	
Milad al-Nabi (Prophet's Birthday)	July	16	-	
Lailat Al-Isra wa Al-Miraj	November	26	-	
Lailat Al-Bara'ah	December	14	-	
1st of Ramadan	December	30	-	

Jewish

	5757		5758	
Purim	March	23	March	12
Pesach (Passover) 1st Day	April	22	April	11
Shavuot (Pentecost) 1st Day	June	11	May	31
	5758		5759	
Rosh Hashanah (New Year)	October	2	September	21
Yom Kippur (Day of Atonement)	October	11	September	20
Succot (Tabernacles)	October	16	October	5
Hanukkah 1st day	December	24	December	14

Sikh

	1997		1998	
Birthday of Guru Gobind Singh Ji				
Baisakhi	January	15	December	25
Martyrdom of Guru Arjan Dev Ji	April	13	April	13
Birthday of GuruNanak Dev Ji	June	9	May	29
Martyrdom of Guru Tegh Bahadur Ji	November	14	November	4
	December	4	November	24

World Standard Times

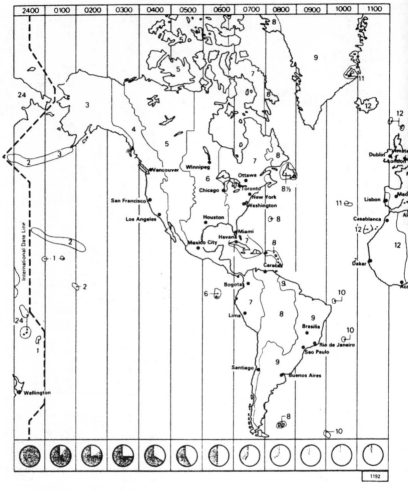

2400	0100	0200	0300	0400	0500	0600	0700	0800	0900	1000	1100

1192

Clock times in various countries

	At noon GMT Standard time	Daylight Saving	
Australia:			
South Australia	2130	2250	Late Oct-early Mar
New South Wales	2200	2300	Late Oct-early Mar
Tasmania	2200	2300	Early Oct-late Mar
Victoria	2200	2300	Late Oct-early Mar
Austria	1300	1400	Late Mar-late Sep
Belgium	1300	1400	Late Mar-late Sep
Bulgaria	1400	1500	Apr-late Sep
Canada:			Early Apr-late Oct
Newfoundland	0830	0930	
Atlantic	0800	0900	

	At noon GMT Standard time	Daylight Saving	
Canada:			Early Apr-late Oct
Central	0600	0700	
Mountain	0500	0600	
Pacific, Yukon	0400	0500	
Czech Republic	1300	1400	Late Mar-late Sep
Denmark	1300	1400	Late Mar-late Sep
Egypt	1400	1500	June-Sep
Finland	1400	1500	Late Mar-late Sep
France	1300	1400	Late Mar-late Sep
Germany	1300	1400	Late Mar-late Sep
Greece	1400	1500	Late Mar-late Sep

166

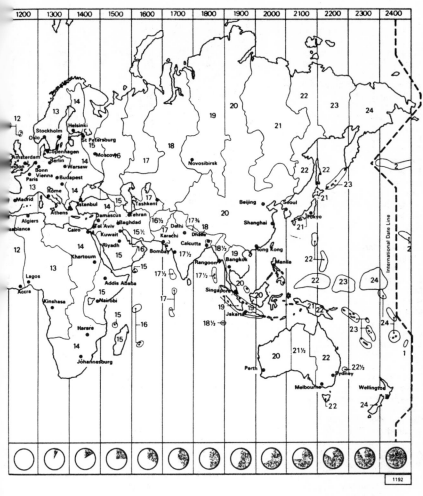

	At noon GMT Standard time	Daylight Saving				At noon GMT Standard time	Daylight Saving	
Iraq	1500	1600	Late Mar-late Sep		Slovak Republic	1300	1400	Late Mar-late Sep
Ireland	1200	1300	Late Mar-late Oct		Spain	1300	1400	Late Mar-late Sep
Italy	1300	1400	Late Mar-late Sep		Sweden	1300	1400	Late Mar-late Sep
Luxembourg	1300	1400	Late Mar-late Sep		Switzerland	1300	1400	Late Mar-late Oct
Netherlands	1300	1400	Late Mar-late Sep		United Kingdom	1200	1300	Late Mar-late Oct
New Zealand	2400	0100	Late Oct-early Mar		United States:			
Norway	1300	1400	Late Mar-late Sep		Eastern	0700	0800	Early Apr-late Oct
Poland	1300	1400	Late Mar-late Sep		Central	0600	0700	
Portugal	1300	1400	Late Mar-late Sep		Mountain	0500	0600	
Russia					Pacific	0400	0500	
St Petersburg, Moscow	1500	1600	Late Mar-late Sep					

167

Notable Dates

	1997	1998	1999
International Holidays			
New Year's Day UK IRL USA CDN AUS NZ HK J	January 1	January 1	January 1
Good Friday UK CDN AUS NZ HK	March 28	April 10	April 2
Easter Monday UK IRL CDN AUS NZ HK	March 31	April 13	April 5
Christmas Day UK IRL USA CDN AUS NZ HK	December 25	December 25	December 25*
Boxing Day UK IRL CDN AUS NZ HK	December 26	December 26*	December 26†
UK and Republic of Ireland			
Mothering Sunday	March 9	March 22	March 14
St Patrick's Day IRL	March 17	March 17	March 17
British Summer Time begins	March 30	March 29‡	March 28‡
May Day Holiday UK	May 5	May 4	May 3
May Holiday IRL	May 5	May 4	May 3
Spring Holiday UK	May 26	May 25	May 31
Holiday IRL	June 2	June 1	June 7
Father's Day	June 15	June 21	June 20
Holiday IRL	August 4	August 3	August 2
Late Summer Holiday UK	August 25	August 31	August 30
British Summer Time ends	October 26	October 25‡	October 31‡
Holiday IRL	October 27	October 26	October 25
Remembrance Sunday	November 9	November 8	November 14
USA and Canada			
Martin Luther King, Jr. Day USA	January 20	January 19	January 18
Presidents' Day USA	February 17	February 16	February 15
Daylight Saving Time begins	April 6	April 5	April 4
Mother's Day	May 11	May 10	May 9
Victoria Day CDN	May 19	May 18	May 24
Memorial Day USA	May 26	May 25	May 31
Father's Day	June 15	June 21	June 20
Canada Day CDN	July 1	July 1	July 1
Independence Day USA	July 4	July 4*	July 4‡
Labor Day USA CDN	September 1	September 7	September 6
Columbus Day USA	October 13	October 12	October 11
Thanksgiving Day CDN	October 13	October 12	October 11
United Nations Day	October 24	October 24	October 24
Daylight Saving Time ends	October 26	October 25	October 31
Veterans Day USA	November 11	November 11	November 11
Remembrance Day CDN	November 11	November 11	November 11
Thanksgiving Day USA	November 27	November 26	November 25
Australia, New Zealand			
and Papua New Guinea			
Holiday NZ	January 2	January 2	January 2*
Devonport Cup TAS	January 8	January 7	January 6
Australia Day AUS	January 26†	January 26	January 26
Hobart Cup Day (South Tasmania)	January 26	January 26	January 26
Waitangi Day NZ	February 6	February 6	February 6*
Hobart Regatta Day (S. Tasmania)	February 11	February 10	February 9
Launceston Cup Day (N. Tasmania)	February 26	February 25	February 24
Labour Day WA	March 3	March 2	March 1
Eight Hour Day TAS	March 3	March 2	March 1
Labour Day VIC	March 10	March 9	March 8
King Island Show TAS	March 11	March 10	March 9
Canberra Day ACT	March 17	March 16	March 15
Easter Saturday AUS not VIC, WA	March 29*	April 11*	April 3*
Summertime ends NSW ACT VIC SA TAS	March 30	March 29	March 28
Easter Tuesday TAS	April 1	April 14	April 6
Anzac Day AUS NZ	April 25	April 25*	April 25†

Notable Dates

	1997	1998	1999
bour Day QLD	May 5	May 4	May 3
y Day NT	May 5	May 4	May 3
other's Day AUS NZ	May 11	May 10	May 9
delaide Cup Day SA	May 19	May 18	May 17
undation Day WA	June 2	June 1	June 7
ueen's Birthday NZ	June 2	June 1	June 7
ueen's Birthday not WA	June 9	June 8	June 14
ueen's Birthday PNG	June 9	June 8	June 14
membrance Day PNG	July 23	July 23	July 23
nk Holiday NSW	August 4	August 3	August 2
cnic Day NT	August 4	August 3	August 3
yal National Show QLD	August 13‡	August 12‡	August 11‡
ther's Day AUS NZ	September 7	September 6	September 5
dependence Day PNG	September 16	September 16	September 16
ueen's Birthday WA	September 29	–	–
urnie Show TAS	October 3	October 2	October 1
immertime begins TAS	October 5	October 4	October 3
bour Day ACT NSW SA	October 6	October 5	October 4
unceston Day TAS	October 9	October 8	October 7
nders Island Show TAS	October 17	October 16	October 15
bart Show TAS	October 23	October 22	October 21
immertime begins NSW ACT VIC SA	October 26	October 25	October 31
bour Day NZ	October 27	October 26	October 25
creation Day (North Tasmania)	November 3	November 2	November 1
elbourne Cup Day (Melb. City)	November 4	November 3	November 2
oclamation Day SA	December 26	December 26*	December 26†

ong Kong‡

	1997	1998	1999
ninese New Year	February 6-9	January 28-30	February 16-18
ing Ming Festival	April 5*	April 5†	April 4
uen Ng Festival	June 9	May 30*	June 18
rthday of HM Queen	June 14*	June 13*	June 12*
oliday	June 16	June 15	June 14
oliday	August 23*	August 29*	August 28*
peration Day	August 25	August 31	August 30
d-Autumn Festival	September 17	September 5	September 25*
ung Yeung Festival	October 10	–	–

apan

	1997	1998	1999
oming of Age Day	January 15	January 15	January 15
ational Foundation Day	February 11	February 11	February 11
ernal Equinox Day	March 20	March 21*	March 21†
reenery Day	April 29	April 29	April 29
onstitution Memorial Day	May 3*	May 3†	May 3
ational Holiday	May 4†	May 4	May 4
hildren's Day	May 5	May 5	May 5
arine Day	July 20†	July 20	July 20
espect for the Aged Day	September 15	September 15	September 15
utumnal Equinox Day	September 23	September 23	September 23
orts Day	October 10	October 10*	October 10†
ulture Day	November 3	November 3	November 3
bour Thanksgiving Day	November 23†	November 23	November 23
mperor's Birthday	December 23	December 23	December 23

ote: When National Holidays fall on Saturday or Sunday, a day may be given in lieu. As this cannot be
ecified at time of going to press, such dates will be marked as follows: * =Saturday   † =Sunday.
=provisional   – =date not available.
l dates are subject to changes and regional and institutional variations.

International Information

Country	Capital	Currency	Population (in millions)	Dialling To	Dialling From	GMT	Air Miles From London
Argentina	Buenos Aires	Peso	32.40	54	00	-3	6,951
Australia	Canberra	Dollar	17.94	61	0011	+8/+10	10,563
Austria	Vienna	Schilling	8.02	43	00	+1	790
Bahrain	Manama	Dinar	0.55	973	00	+3	3,154
Belgium	Brussels	Franc	10.07	32	00	+1	217
Bolivia	La Paz	Boliviano	6.40	591	00	-4	6,780
Brazil	Brasilia	Cruzeiro	156.30	55	00	-2/-5	5,767
Bulgaria	Sofia	Lev	8.50	359	00	+2	1,258
Canada	Ottawa	Dollar	29.25	1	011	-3½/2/-8	3,321
Chile	Santiago	Peso	138.00	56	00	-4	7,493
China	Beijing	Yuan	1200.00	86	00	+8	5,063
Colombia	Bogota	Peso	36.00	57	90	-5	5,294
Cuba	Havana	Peso	10.90	53	119	-5	4,662
Denmark	Copenhagen	Krone	5.18	45	00	+1	608
Egypt	Cairo	Pound	59.00	20	00	+2	2,185
Estonia	Tallinn	Kroon	1.50	372	800	+2	1,118
Finland	Helsinki	Markka	5.08	358	990	+2	1,148
France	Paris	Franc	57.22	33	19	+1	215
Germany	Berlin	Mark	81.08	49	00	+1	588
Ghana	Accra	Cedi	17.00	233	00	GMT	3,117
Greece	Athens	Drachma	10.26	30	00	+2	1,500
Hong Kong	Victoria	Dollar	6.15	852	001	+8	5,990
Hungary	Budapest	Forint	10.28	36	00	+1	923
Iceland	Reykjavik	Króna	0.27	354	00	GMT	1,175
India	New Delhi	Rupee	846.00	91	00	+5½	4,169
Indonesia	Jakarta	Rupiah	189.00	62	00	+7/+9	7,287
Ireland (Rep. of)	Dublin	Punt	3.53	353	00	GMT	279
Israel	Jerusalem/ Tel Aviv	Shekel	5.00	972	00	+2	2,219
Italy	Rome	Lira	56.78	39	00	+1	895
Japan	Tokyo	Yen	124.76	81	001	+9	5,956
Kenya	Nairobi	Shilling	26.00	254	00	+3	4,246
Korea (Rep. of)	Seoul	Won	0.68	82	00	+9	5,663
Latvia	Riga	Lat	2.55	371	00	+2	1,035

International Information

British Embassy Overseas	Foreign Embassy in London
Dr. Luis Agote 2412, 1425 Buenos Aires Tel: Buenos Aires 803-7070/1	53, Hans Place, SW1X 0LA (0171) 584 6494
British High Commission, Commonwealth Avenue, Yarralumia, Canberra ACT 2600	High Commission, Australia House, Strand, WC2B 4LA (0171) 379 4334
Jaurèsgasse 12, 1030 Vienna	18 Belgrave Mews West, SW1X 8HU (0171) 235 3731
21 Government Avenue, Manama 306, PO Box 114 Tel: Manama 534404	98 Gloucester Road, SW7 4AU (0171) 370 5132
rue d'Arlon 85, 1040 Brussels	103 Eaton Square, SW1W 9AB (0171) 235 5422
Avenida Arce 2732 (Casilla 694) La Paz Tel: La Paz 357 424	106 Eaton Square, SW1W 9AD (0171) 235 2257/4248
Setor de Embaicadus Sul, Quadra 801, Ycep 70.408, Brasilia Tel: Brasilia 225-2710	32 Green Street, W1Y 4AT (0171) 499 0877
Boulevard Vassil Levski 65-67, Sofia 1000 Tel: Sofia 492 3361	186-8 Queen's Gate, SW7 5HL (0171) 584 9400/9433
British High Commission, 80 Elgin Street, Ottawa K1P 5K7	High Commission, 1 Grosvenor Square, W1X 0AB (0171) 258 6600
Avenida El Basque Norte 0125, Casilla 72-P, Santiago 9 Tel: Santiago 231 3737	12 Devonshire Street, W1N 2DS (0171) 580 6392
11 Guang Hua Lu, Jian Guo Men Wai, Beijing 100 600	49-51 Portland Place, W1N 3AH (0171) 636 9375
Torre Propaganda Sancho, Calle 98, No. 9-03 Piso 4, Bogotá Tel: Bogotá 218 511	Flat 3A, 3 Hans Crescent, SW1X 0LR (0171) 589 9177/5037
e 7 ma Y17, Miramar, Havana Tel: Havana 331771	167 High Holborn, WC1V 6PA (0171) 240 2488
36-40 Kasetelvej, DK-2100 Copenhagen Ø	55 Sloane Street, SW1X 9SR (0171) 333 0200
Ahmed Ragheb Street, Garden City, Cairo Tel: Cairo 354 0850	26 South Street, W1Y 8EL (0171) 499 2401
Kewtmanni 20, Tallinn EE0100 Tel: Tallinn 6313353	16 Hyde Park Gate, SW7 5DG (0171) 589 3428
Itäinen Puistotie 17, 00140 Helsinki	38 Chesham Place, SW1X 8HW (0171) 838 6200
35 rue du Faubourg St Honoré, 75383 Paris Cedex 08	58 Knightsbridge, SW1X 7JT (0171) 201 1000
Friedrich-Ebert-Allee 77, 53113 Bonn	23 Belgrave Square, SW1X 8PZ (0171) 824 1300
PO Box 296, Osu Link, Accra Tel: Accra 221 665	104 Highgate Hill, N6 5HE (0181) 342 8686
1 Ploutarchou Street, 10675 Athens	1a Holland Park, W1I 3TP (0171) 229 3850
British Council Representative, Easey Commercial Building 225 Hennessy Road, Wanchai, Hong Kong	Government Office, 6 Grafton Street, W1X 3LB (0171) 499 9821
Harmincad Utca 6, Budapest V	35 Eaton Place, SW1X 8BY (0171) 235 4048
Laufásvegur 49, 101 Reykjavik Tel: Reykjavik 551 15883/4	1 Eaton Terrace, SW1W 8EY (0171) 730 5131/2
Chawakyapuri, New Delhi 110021 Tel: New Delhi 872 161	India House, Aldwych, London WC2B 4NA (0171) 836 8484
Jalan M. H. Thamrin 75, Jakarta 10310 Tel: Jakarta 330904	38 Grosvenor Square, London W1X 9AD (0171) 499 7661
31 Merrion Road, Dublin 4	17 Grosvenor Place, SW1X 7HR (0171) 235 2171
192 Hayarkon Street, Tel Aviv 63405 Tel: Tel Aviv 524 9171	2 Palace Green, Kensington, W8 4QB (0171) 957 9500
Via XX Settembre 80A, 00187 Rome	14 Three Kings Yard, Davies Street, W1Y 2EH (0171) 312 2200
No 1 Ichiban-cho, Chiyoda-ku, Tokyo 102	101-104 Piccadilly, W1V 9FN (0171) 465 6500
Bruce House, Standard Street, PO Box 30465, Nairobi Tel: Nairobi 335944	45 Portland Place, W1N 4AS (0171) 636 2371
No 4, Chung-Dong, Chung-Ku, Seoul 100 Tel: Seoul 735 7341/3	60 Buckingham Gate, SW1E 6AJ (0171) 227 5500
5 Alunana lela Street, Riga LV1010 Tel: Riga 733 8126	45 Nottingham Place, W1M 3FE (0171) 312 0040

International Information

Country	Capital	Currency	Population (in millions)	Dialling To	Dialling From	GMT	Air Miles From London
Lithuania	Vilnius	Litas	3.75	370	00	+2	1,070
Luxembourg	Luxembourg	Franc	0.40	352	00	+1	311
Malaysia	Kuala Lumpur	Ringgit	19.96	60	00	+8	6,557
Mexico	Mexico City	Peso	81.00	52	00	-6/-8	5,543
Netherlands	Amsterdam	Guilder	15.24	31	00	+1	230
New Zealand	Wellington	Dollar	3.49	64	00	+12	11,692
Nigeria	Abuja	Naira	115.66	234	009	+1	3,107
Norway	Oslo	Krone	4.32	47	095	+1	722
Pakistan	Islamabad	Rupee	84.00	92	00	+5	3,755
Papua New Guinea	Port Moresby	Kina	4.25	675	00	+10	9,756
Paraguay	Asunción	Guarani	4.90	595	00	-4	5,567
Peru	Lima	Sol	22.30	51	00	-5	6,580
Philippines	Manila	Peso	66.20	63	00	+8	7,907
Poland	Warsaw	Zloty	38.30	48	00	+1	912
Portugal	Lisbon	Escudo	9.86	351	00	+1	972
Romania	Bucharest	Leu	22.80	40	00	+2	1,298
Russian Federation	Moscow	Rouble	148.30	7	810	+2/+12	1,557
Saudi Arabia	Riyadh	Rial	17.00	966	00	+3	3,073
Singapore	-	Dollar	3.00	65	00	+9	6,748
South Africa	Pretoria	Rand	40.00	27	00	+2	5,640
Spain	Madrid	Peseta	38.87	34	07	+1	773
Sweden	Stockholm	Krona	8.75	46	009	+1	908
Switzerland	Bern	Franc	6.91	41	00	+1	476
Taiwan	Taipei	Dollar	21.00	886	00	+8	6,316
Thailand	Bangkok	Baht	58.30	66	00	+7	5,919
Turkey	Ankara	Lira	56.50	90	00	+2	1,720
UAE	Abu Dhabi	Dirham	2.40	971	00	+4	3,409
UK	London	Pound	58.4	44	00	GMT	–
USA	Washington DC	Dollar	259.68	1	011	-5/-10	3,665
Venezuela	Caracas	Bolívar	21.40	58	00	-4	4,657
Vietnam	Hanoi	Dông	72.50	84	00	+7	6,265
Zaire	Kinshasa	Zaire	39.88	243	00	+1	3,876
Zimbabwe	Harare	Dollar	10.40	263	00	+2	5,159

International Information

British Embassy Overseas	Foreign Embassy in London
2 Antakalnio, 2055 Vilnius Tel: Vilnius 2222070	84 Gloucester Place, W1H 3HN (0171) 486 6401
14 Boulevard F. D. Roosevelt, L-2450 Luxembourg Ville	27 Wilton Crescent, SW1X 8SD (0171) 235 6961
British High Commission, 185 Jalan Ampang, (PO Box 11030) 50450 Kuala Lumpur	High Commission, 45 Belgrave Square, SW1X 7HR (0171) 235 8033
Callé Rio Lerma 71, Colonia Cuauhtémoc, 06500 Mexico City Tel: Mexico City 207 2089	42 Hertford Street, W1Y 7TF (0171) 499 8586
Lange Voorhout 10, The Hague, 2514 ED	38 Hyde Park Gate, SW7 5DP (0171) 584 5040
British High Commission, 44 Hill Street, (PO Box 1812) Wellington 1	High Commission, NZ House, 80 Haymarket, SW1Y 4TQ (0171) 930 8422
British High Commission, Shehu Shangari Way (North) Maitama, Abuja	High Commission, 9 Northumberland Avenue, WC2N 5BX (0171) 839 1244
Thomas Heftyesgate 8, 0244 Oslo	25 Belgrave Square, SW1X 8QD (0171) 235 7151
Diplomatic Encave, Romna 5, (PO Box 1122) Islamabad, Tel: Islamabad 822131/5	35-36 Lowndes Square, SW1X 9JN (0171) 235 2044
PO Box 212, Waigani NCP 131, Port Moresby Tel: Port Moresby 2516773	3rd floor, 14 Waterloo Place, SW1R 4AR (0171) 930 0922/7
Calle Presidente Franco 706 (PO Box 404) Asunción Tel: Asunción 444472	Braemar Lodge, Cornwall Gardens, SW7 4AQ (0171) 937 1253
Edificio El Pacifico, Washington, Pizo 12, Plaza Washington (PO Box 854) Lima 100 Tel: Lima 334 735	52 Sloane Street, SW1X 9SP (0171) 235 1917/2545
Locsin Building, 6752 Ayala Avenue, Corner Makati Avenue, 1226 Makati, Metro Manila (PO Box 2927 MCPO)	9A Palace Green, W8 4QE (0171) 937 1600
I Aleja Róz, 00-556 Warsaw	47 Portland Place, W1N 3AG (0171) 580 4324
35-37 Rua de S. Domingos à Lapa, 1200 Lisbon	11 Belgrave Square, SW1X 8PP (0171) 235 5331
24 Strade Jules Michelet, 70154, Bucharest Tel: Bucharest 3120 303	Arundel House, 4 Palace Green, W8 4QD (0171) 937 9666
Moscow 72, Sosiskaya Naberexhnaya 14	13 Kensington Palace Gardens, W8 4QX (0171) 229 3628
PO Box 94351 Riyadh 11693 Tel: Riyadh 4880077	30 Charles Street, W1X 7PM (0171) 917 3000
Tanglin Road, Singapore 247919 Tel: Singapore 473 9333	9 Wilton Crescent, SW1X 8SA (0171) 235 8315
255 Hill Street, Pretoria 002 Tel: Pretoria 433121	S Africa House, Trafalgar Square, SC2N 5DP (0171) 930 4488
Calle de Fernando el Santo, 16, 28010 Madrid	39 Chesham Place, SW1X 8QA (0171) 235 5555
Skarpögatan 6-8, S115 93 Stockholm	11 Montagu Place, W1H 2AL (0171) 917 6400
Thunstrasse 50, 3005 Berne	16-18 Montagu Place, W1H 2BQ (0171) 723 0701
Tom Buchanan, 7th floor, Fu Key Building, 99 Jen Ai Road, Section 2, Taipei Tel: Taipei 10625	50 Grosvenor Gardens, SW1W 0EB
Thanon Witthayn, Bangkok 10330 Tel: Bangkok 253 01919	1-3 Yorkshire House, Grosvenor Crescent SW1X 7EP (0171) 259 5005
Sehit Ersan Caddesi 45/A, Cankaya, Ankara Tel: Ankara 4686230	43 Belgrave Square, SW1X 8PA (0171) 393 0202
PO Box 248, Abu Dhabi Tel: Abu Dhabi 326600	30 Princes Gate, SW7 1PT (0171) 581 1281
–	–
3100 Massachusetts Avenue, NW, Washington DC 20008	24 Grosvenor Square, W1A 1AE (0171) 499 9000
Apartado 1246, Caracas 1010-A Tel: Caracas 9934111	1 Cromwell Road, SW7 2HW (0171) 836 7755
16 Pho Ly Thuong Kiet, Hanoi Tel: Hanoi 252 349	12-14 Victoria Road, W8 5RD (0171) 937 1912 8564
Avenue des Trois 'Z' Gombe, Kinshasa	26 Chesham Place, SW1X 8HH (0171) 235 6137
Corner House, Samora Machel Avenue, (PO Box 4490) Harare Tel: Harare 793 781	Zimbabwe House, 429 Strand, WC2R 0SA (0171) 9371912/8564

Acknowledgements

I would like to thank a whole group of people without whom I would not have been able to attempt this book...

Brothers **Mat** and **Rob**, the Bruton sisters – **Alison** and **Katie, Claire Eely-Sedding** (and of course **Mrs.D!**), **Helena Sampson, Jane Stuart, Colin Pidgeon, Jason Race** and **John Taylor** for help with the computer problems, **Rob LeMare, SJA Canavan, Jerry Tate, Martin 'Props' Holland,** little **Cathy Cobley, Lyndsey Underhill, Philippa Symonds, Marie Robey, Dawn Howell, Ed** and **Penny, Kirsten Whiting, Steve Butterworth** for his timely advice, **Nina** and **Tania** – my Canadian Girlies, **Ed** and **Jo** for their kindness and so subsequent inspiration (and forgiveness for my 'blunder' at their wedding – bit of a classic though!), **Ben Slater** my Diabetic literary master, **Penny Bell** for her guidance. **Alan Bettles** for accompanying me during those long hours at the computer, and of course **Suffolk College** (and **Gillian** at reception) for the use of their computers and allowing me to finish this book off. And my proof readers: **Richard 'oofy' Mortimer** for a fantastic job way beyond the call of duty, **Chris Welburn, Steve Freeman, Danielle O'Malley, Amanda Harris, Dan Woods, Simon Marsh, Stephanie Jones** and **Oliver Baxter** (the last three who have taken the book quite literally, and who at the time of publication are off travelling the world... see, it does work!). Cartoonist: **Dave Upson** – I'm sure you'll agree with me that this lad has a great talent, and am very thankful for his enthusiasm and co-operation, and his determination to step forward and take up the challenge.

Special mentions also to **Suzie Money** – a remarkable woman who gave me the invaluable confidence I needed. **Marcus Orlovsky** and **Nena Dowse** – unknown to them, they have been major influences on my thoughts and way of life – many thanks. **Jeremy Greenwood**, the publisher. I've still got a lot to learn and a long way to go. You gave me 'the start'. Thanks.

Subject index

Accidents	52
Advice (bad)	62, 109, 129
Appendicitis	135, 159
Australia	2, 12, 73, 137
Backpack	19, 65, 121
Banks	96
Bargaining	121, 139
Beaches	122
Bike hire	141
Black market	97
Blondes	70
Books	31, **162**
Boyfriends	77
Budgeting	12,14,30,80,82,93,128
Buses	2
Cameras	144
Camping	82, 124
Cars	122
Changing plans	56, 127
Chilling out	125
Coming Home	4, **152**
Companions	76, 81
Confidence	65
Credit cards	97, 107, 126
Culture shock	58, 69, 127
Currency	95
Dangerous countries	84
Day bag	25
Decisions	**5**

Dehydration	128
Delayed flights	132
Diabetics	49
Diet	128
Dress codes	70
Drugs	129
Eating	128
Embassies	47, 130
Emergencies	**46**
Emergency Money Transfer	105
Exhibitionists	81
Female Solo	**61**
Female travel tips	61-74
Fijian, Experience	57
Finances	**92**
First Aid (+Course)	24, 131, 134
Flexibility	11
Flights	131
Food	128, 132
Fruit	128
Gifts	133
Girlfriends	77
Going with a Friend	**75**
Ground rules	80, 83
Guidebooks	132, 162
Gung-Ho travellers	132
Hairdressers	134
Hassles	69
Health	**46**, 134

175

Hitch-Hiking | 111

Illness | 53, 134, 142,
Independence | 55, 59, 61
Injections | 137
Insurance | 10, 135-137
International Debit Cards | 98
Itchy Feet | 57, 155
Itineraries | 10

Jobs | 73, 93, 137

Keeping in touch | 37

Languages | 140
Laws | 148
Letters | 40
Locals | 108, 125, 139, 150
Loneliness | 54-56, 60

Male Solo | 54
Mechanics | 141
Medication worries | 47
Millets | 19, 25, 65, 121
Money and Finances | 92
Money (carrying) | 107-109
Money changing | 96
Money (saving) | 94
Money transfer | 102-106
Motivation | 6, 14, 75
Muggings | 63, 85, 142

Musical instruments | 141

Nerves | 14

Organising Yourself | 13, 36, 76, 81

Packing | 18, 65
Parents | 32, 94, 106
Passport | 23, 142
Patience | 143
Phone calls | 44
Photography | 143
PIN numbers | 145
Planning tips | 16, 64, 81

Police | 146
Postcards | 44
Posting Items | 148
Post Restante | 40
Protection | 84, 146

Queen | 148

Relatives | 43
Round the World tickets | 10-11
Rules | 148

Safety | **84**, 110
Saving money | 94
Shipping items | 148
Sleeping Bags | 149
Sleeping rough | 115, 149
So Why Travel? | **1**
STA Travel | 8
Sun | 24, 135

Taping yourself | 45
Tax | 94
Telephone Numbers & Addresses | **163**
Things To Do Checklist | **158**
Tickets | 12
Tips, Hints and Problems | **120**
Travel agent | 6-8, 158
Travel bug | 57, 155
Travellers cheques | 99
Travellers Connections | 42
Travelling around | 56
Trouble/Thieves | 89
Trains | 150

Universities | 150

Vegetarians | 150
Voice Mail | 42

Weather cycles | 6
Wedding ring | 66
Western Union Money Transfer | 105
Wildlife | 125, 150
Work | 73, 93, 137

millets

 ^m

THE OUTDOORS STORE

OFFER YOU A 10% DISCOUNT

As Britain's biggest retailer of outdoor gear, we've got
everything you'll need to make your trip go smoothly.
Choose from our wide range of rucksacks and daysacks,
boots and shoes, sleeping bags and camp mats,
plus hundreds of useful accessories.

Our expert staff will be happy to help you choose
which item best suits your needs.

If you can't find everything you are looking for
you may be able to place an order through our
Special Order Line; ask in store for details.

With 157 stores nationwide there's bound to be one
near you. Call 01604 441111 to find out where it is.

We stock these and other brands

Bring this book with you to receive your discount
at any Millets store.

178

179

We love hearing from you and think you'd like to hear from us.

When..... is the right time to see reindeer in Finland?

Where....can you hear the best palm-wine music in Ghana?

How....... do you get from Asunción to Areguá by steam train?

What...... is the best way to see India?

For the answer to these and many other questions read

- Lonely Planet's FREE quarterly Newsletter

Every issue is packed with up-to-date travel news and advice including:

- a letter from Lonely Planet co-founders Tony and Maureen Wheeler
- go behind the scenes on the road with a Lonely Planet author
- feature article on an important and topical travel issue
- a selection of recent letters from travellers
- details on forthcoming Lonely Planet promotions
- complete list of Lonely Planet products

To join our mailing list contact:

Lonely Planet, The Barley Mow Centre, 10 Barley Mow Passage, Chiswick, London W4 4PH. Tel: (0181) 742 3161 Fax: (0181) 742 2772
e-mail: 100413.3551@compuserve.com
For 2000 pages of news, views and updates: www.lonelyplanet.com

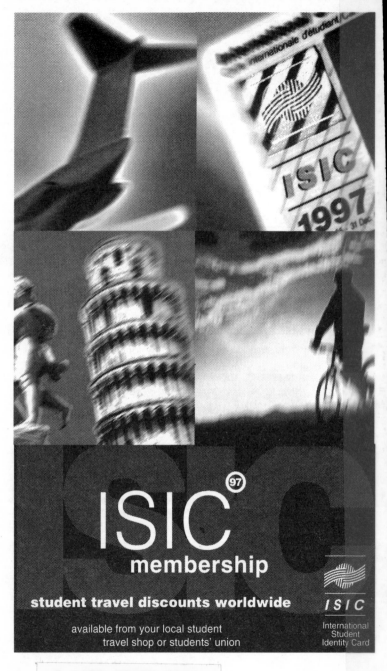

ISIC °97

membership

student travel discounts worldwide

available from your local student
travel shop or students' union

ISIC

International
Student
Identity Card